Praise for *Microsoft Visual Studio Tips . . .*

*"If Visual Studio is the King of IDEs, then Sara Ford is our Q[...]
of the very best Visual Studio tips and tricks and sprinkled t[...]
insight, historical context and humor. Recommended!"*

Scott Hanselman, Microsoft Dev[...]

"More good code faster! That's what Visual Studio is meant to help you do, but how do you become a MASTER PILOT? Sara's book "Microsoft Visual Studio Tips" is just chock full of time saving nuggets. I especially like the "Sara Aside" insertions through the book. Read it and increase your development productivity every day."

Joe Stagner, Microsoft Senior Program Manager

"Every VS developer can find time-saving tips in this new book. Adopt them and spend more time 'in the zone' as a result!"

Scott Wiltamuth, Microsoft Visual Studio Partner Program Manager

"Throughout this book, Sara Ford exposes and demonstrates hundreds of Visual Studio features and capabilities that can help conserve your most precious resource—your time."

Rob Caron, Microsoft Developer Marketing

"Even those of us who work directly on Visual Studio are rarely familiar with all the capabilities of the product, and especially the shortcuts that access those capabilities quickly, so a source of tips like these is highly valuable and most welcome!"

Pat Brenner, Microsoft Senior Software Design Engineer

"Sara Ford's energy, expertise, and enthusiasm have made her everyone's favorite source of in-formation about the Visual Studio IDE. She has an endless store of knowledge on how to be more productive when using Visual Studio, and in this book she freely shares that knowledge with us."

Charlie Calvert, Microsoft C# Community Program Manager

"Sara's tips show off every nook and cranny of Visual Studio, some productivity features I didn't even know existed, and are indispensible for beginner and advanced programmers alike."

Beth Massi, Microsoft Visual Studio Community Program Manager

"This book is a treasure chest of useful gems that has already saved me time when I'm working with code! Just from the first chapter, I learned a new tip that I'm going to start using today."

Karen Liu, Lead Program Manager, Microsoft Visual C#

"Excellent coverage of the Visual Studio IDE from someone who knows it inside out!"

Lisa Feigenbaum, Program Manager, Microsoft Visual Studio Languages

i

Microsoft®

Microsoft®
Visual Studio® Tips

Sara Ford

PUBLISHED BY
Microsoft Press
A Division of Microsoft Corporation
One Microsoft Way
Redmond, Washington 98052-6399

Library of Congress Control Number: 2008935423

Printed and bound in the United States of America.

1 2 3 4 5 6 7 8 9   QWT   3 2 1 0 9 8

Distributed in Canada by H.B. Fenn and Company Ltd.

A CIP catalogue record for this book is available from the British Library.

Microsoft Press books are available through booksellers and distributors worldwide. For further information about international editions, contact your local Microsoft Corporation office or contact Microsoft Press International directly at fax (425) 936-7329. Visit our Web site at www.microsoft.com/mspress. Send comments to mspinput@microsoft.com.

Microsoft, Microsoft Press, DataTips, IntelliSense, MSDN, Visual Basic, Visual C#, Visual C++, Visual InterDev, Visual J++, Visual Studio, Windows, and Windows Vista are either registered trademarks or trademarks of the Microsoft group of companies. Other product and company names mentioned herein may be the trademarks of their respective owners.

The example companies, organizations, products, domain names, e-mail addresses, logos, people, places, and events depicted herein are fictitious. No association with any real company, organization, product, domain name, e-mail address, logo, person, place, or event is intended or should be inferred.

This book expresses the author's views and opinions. The information contained in this book is provided without any express, statutory, or implied warranties. Neither the authors, Microsoft Corporation, nor its resellers, or distributors will be held liable for any damages caused or alleged to be caused either directly or indirectly by this book.

Acquisitions Editor: Ben Ryan
Developmental Editor: Devon Musgrave
Project Editor: Melissa von Tschudi-Sutton
Editorial Production: ICC Macmillan, Inc.
Cover: Tom Draper Design

Body Part No. X15-16984

To Beulah "Maw Maw" Rossignol. You would have loved this.

And to my mentor Sam Ramji for teaching me how to take a stand, especially for myself.

All author book royalties will be used to create a scholarship fund for anyone living in the author's hometown of Waveland, Mississippi, which was destroyed during Hurricane Katrina. Scholarship preference will be given to math and computer science majors.

The following photo was taken on August 3, 2008, in front of Waveland City Hall, *three years after* the hurricane.

"From the people of Waveland: In appreciation and gratitude to all who gave of their time, energy, and money to help us recover from Hurricane Camille. On August 17, 1969 our city was devastated, but those who cared came to her rescue."

Throughout her life, the author has always had a quest for knowledge. Now, sales from this book will be used to help others pursue their own quests.

For more information regarding the Save Waveland Scholarship Fund, please contact the Mississippi Gulf Coast Community College Foundation, INC, PO Box 99, Perkinston, MS 39573 or visit *https://www.mgccc.edu/creditcard.htm* for direct donations.

Contents at a Glance

Table of Contents

What do you think of this book? We want to hear from you!

Microsoft is interested in hearing your feedback so we can continually improve our books and
learning resources for you. To participate in a brief online survey, please visit:

www.microsoft.com/learning/booksurvey

What do you think of this book? We want to hear from you!

Microsoft is interested in hearing your feedback so we can continually improve our books and learning resources for you. To participate in a brief online survey, please visit:

www.microsoft.com/learning/booksurvey

Foreword

As I write this, the world is converging on Beijing, China for the 2008 Summer Olympic Games. The athletes have spent years tuning their bodies and movements for optimal efficiency and effectiveness in preparation for this moment. Those wearing the gold medals for many events will be determined by mere fractions of a second.

Although medals aren't typically awarded for accomplishing your programming tasks the fastest, the book you hold in your hands can help you use Visual Studio more efficiently and effectively. Many of the tips in this book will only save you a few seconds or less; however, as developers, we all know that a routine performed thousands of times can benefit from even the smallest optimization.

Throughout this book, Sara brings to light capabilities within Visual Studio you may never have known existed, or have long since forgotten. Despite spending nearly ten years at Microsoft in and around Visual Studio, Sara's blog expose holes in my knowledge. Whether you've been using Visual Studio since the 1990s, or you are installing it for the first time, you will find value on the pages that follow.

It wasn't until I read the manuscript for this book that I came to realize the role I played in Sara's Visual Studio Tip of the Day series and this book. I am happy to have had the opportunity to share some of this experience with her. It was inspiring (but not surprising) to learn that Sara is taking the proceeds from this book, which is founded on the principle of helping developers make better use of Visual Studio, to help others in her hometown pursue careers in software.

"Go, Sara, go!"

Rob Caron

Redmond, Washington

August, 2008

Introduction

This book contains the best 251 tips for mastering the ins and outs of the Visual Studio environment. Imagine every Tools Options setting that's generic across any language explained using the simplest examples. Imagine every nook and cranny of the core environment illustrated for you to explore. The tips in this book explore these aspects of the Integrated Development Environment (IDE), so you don't have to imagine anymore.

Before you jump straight in to the tips, please note: *It is imperative you know which development settings you are using, so you know which keyboard shortcuts to use.*

I wrote these tips using the Generic Development Settings and the U.S. English keyboard layout. You can use Tip 6.1 to find out which development settings you are using and Tip 6.2 to reset your settings, in case you want to follow along directly word for word and keyboard shortcut for keyboard shortcut.

If you want to follow along using your current settings, please read Tip 0.0, found at the end of this introduction, to know which keyboard shortcuts to use. And yes, I was clearly a math major in college, since I start counting at 0.

How This Book Happened

In March of 2005, I shared an office with Sean Laberee, the program manager for the Visual Studio core editor. While I was walking out the office to grab lunch one day, the words "Tip of the Day" on his monitor caught my eye. I didn't want Sean to think I was intentionally reading his monitor, but at the same time, I was too intrigued by the idea to just let it go.

When I got back, I asked him about this "Tip of the Day." He explained his idea of having these "did you know" tips on the Visual Studio start page. I suggested that we use my blog to experiment with an editor tip of the day for a few months. I had recently joined the editor team as a software tester, and I was surprised how much functionality existed that I didn't know about.

Now enter Rob Caron, a marketing manager for Visual Studio. Rob noticed the experiment on the MSDN RSS feed and inspired me to go above and beyond by running a weekly tip series on more aspects of Visual Studio. He gave the tips much love by featuring them on the Visual Studio home page.

I had to share my excitement seeing the tips on the product's Web site, so I called home on Saturday, August 27, 2005, to tell my family to check this out. But the excitement was very short-lived. My mom informed me that "the big one" was out there in the Gulf of Mexico, heading toward New Orleans. I said, "Oh really? I haven't been following hurricane season this year. What's the name?" I would never hear the name Katrina quite the same again.

In Spring of 2007, after having made the career switch from software design engineer in test to program management, I decided I would try the weekly tip series again for Visual Studio 2008. Again, enter Rob Caron. He says, "You know, a tip of the day would really rock." I am completely powerless to say no to big challenges.

The idea of writing a book and donating the author royalties was always in the back of my head during the Visual Studio 2008 "Tip of the Day" series, given how I had just left the Visual Studio team to join the CodePlex team. Fortunately, thanks to all the requests to write a book from my blog readers over the next several months, I realized the time had come.

Who This Book Is For

The tips presented in this book are targeted at the core environment functionality of Visual Studio, so they are generic across any programming language. To create these tips, I broke down these generic feature areas of the IDE into very small pieces of functionality. Hence, some of the tips will explore trivial aspects of Visual Studio whereas others will explore the less-obvious, more-obscure areas. In other words, my goal is to capture all the ins and outs of Visual Studio so we can all share the same baseline knowledge of how the IDE works.

How This Book Is Organized

The chapters correspond to how we, the Visual Studio Core QA Team, categorized the feature areas internally for the Visual Studio 2005 product cycle. Some feature areas, like the editor, were so big that I had to break them out into several chapters. Other chapters seemed to flow better when based on functionality, like the tool windows versus dialog boxes sections in Chapter 5 and Chapter 6.

Tips are numbered sequentially within each chapter. For example, Chapter 3 contains 23 tips, so you'll find the tips ordered as Tip 3.1, Tip 3.2, all the way to Tip 3.23. We figured it is easier to refer to a tip as Tip 3.23 rather than Tip 103, if we numbered sequentially throughout the book, or Tip 3.4.3, if we broke them down into subsections.

Additionally, you'll see my "Sara Asides" throughout these tips, where I share something personal in regard to the tip, whether it is a stroll down memory lane, an FYI about how the feature was tested, a story about writing the tip for the "Tip of the Day" series, or a rant about Seattle weather.

Lastly, I decided to give ya'll some good New Orleans–style lagniappe—a little something extra on the side, free of charge. I've included appendices where I share more tips on things beyond Visual Studio, like writing a "Tip of the Day" series, surviving as a software tester, and stories about creating the IDE from those who were there.

System Requirements

This book is optimized for Microsoft Visual Studio 2005 and Microsoft Visual Studio 2008. All tips will work in Visual Studio 2005 unless otherwise noted within the tip that it is a feature specific for Visual Studio 2008.

Contact the Author

You can visit the corresponding "Tip of the Day" series located on my blog at *http://blogs.msdn.com/saraford* to see additional commentary from readers.

 Note If you are looking for support regarding a keyboard shortcut, a missing piece of the user interface, or a command that doesn't seem available, please refer to Tip 0.0, Tip 6.1, and Tip 6.2. I wrote these tips using the General Development Settings, so it is possible that the development settings you are using have modified the UI slightly.

Support for This Book

Every effort has been made to ensure the accuracy of this book and companion content. Microsoft Press provides corrections for books through the Web at the following address:

http://www.microsoft.com/mspress/support/search.aspx

To connect directly to Microsoft Help and Support to enter a query regarding a question or issue you may have, go to the following address:

http://support.microsoft.com

If you have comments, questions, or ideas regarding the book or companion content or if you have questions that are not answered by querying the Knowledge Base, please send them to Microsoft Press using either of the following methods:

E-mail:

mspinput@microsoft.com

Postal mail:

Microsoft Press
Attn: *Microsoft Visual Studio Tips* editor
One Microsoft Way
Redmond, WA 98052-6399

Please note that product support is not offered through the preceding mail addresses. For support information, please visit the Microsoft Product Support Web site at

http://support.microsoft.com

Tip 0.0: How to Look Up, Change, or Create Visual Studio Keyboard Shortcuts

> **Sara Aside** Seriously, I cannot stress enough how imperative it is that you know which development settings you are using, in order to know the right keyboard shortcuts for these commands. This "tip" is so critical that I call it Tip 0.0. I really want you to have a good time with this book, so please read this tip before continuing your adventures in Visual Studio Tips Land.

What Will This Keyboard Shortcut Do?

To find out what command a keyboard shortcut is bound to:

1. Go to the Tools–Options dialog box and navigate to the Environment–Keyboard page.

2. In the Press Shortcut Keys edit box, press the keyboard shortcut you are inquiring about.

The Shortcuts For Selected Command combo box displays the associated command(s). If there are no commands associated with the keybinding, the combo box is empty. Please be sure to drop down the list if there are multiple commands associated with that command.

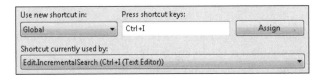

What Is the Keyboard Shortcut for This Command?

To view a keyboard shortcut for a given command:

1. Go to the Tools–Options dialog box and navigate to the Environment–Keyboard page.

2. Type the command name in the Show Commands Containing edit box or select the command from the list box.

The Shortcuts For Selected Command combo box will display the keyboard shortcut, if it exists.

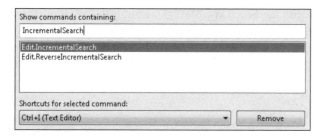

How to Create or Change a Keyboard Shortcut

To change or create a keyboard shortcut for a given command:

1. Go to the Tools–Options dialog box and navigate to the Environment–Keyboard page.

2. Type the command name in the Show Commands Containing edit box or select the command from the list box.

3. In the Press Shortcut Keys edit box, press the keyboard shortcut you want to associate with the currently selected command. The Press Shortcut Keys edit box will display the keybinding you pressed for your confirmation.

4. Click Assign.

If there's a conflict, the Shortcut Currently Used By combo box will show the conflict. Click Assign to override the conflict.

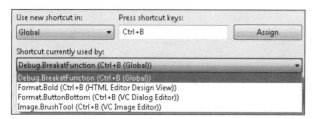

Note that there are different scopes. The Use New Shortcut In combo box shows the current scope for a given keyboard shortcut. For example, keyboard shortcuts assigned in the Text Editor scope will work only when focus is in the editor, regardless of whether you are editing a plain text file or a C# file. If there's ever a conflict between a keyboard shortcut in the global scope and any other scope, the more specific scope wins, and that command executes.

Where Are the Keyboard Shortcut Reference Posters?

The Visual Studio team provides some keyboard shortcut reference posters, which are based on the standard U.S. English keyboard layout as shown at *http://www.microsoft.com/globaldev/keyboards/kbdus.htm*.

Note this book explores many of the less-commonly known aspects of the IDE. So it is still a good idea to be familiar with Tip 0.0, in the case that these posters don't cover a specific command or keyboard shortcut.

Keyboard Shortcut Reference Posters for Visual Studio:

- Visual Basic 2008 keybindings: *http://go.microsoft.com/?linkid=9323901*
- Visual C# 2008 keybindings: *http://go.microsoft.com/?linkid=9323900*
- Visual C++ 2008 keybindings: *http://go.microsoft.com/?linkid=9323899*

Acknowledgements

This Acknowledgement section is an experiment to prove whether my theory is correct that the sooner I start writing thank you notes, the fewer people I'll forget to thank. I started writing this section when I formatted my very first chapter. If I have forgotten to name my first-born child after you (alongside all the others listed below), it is only because of the insomnia I subjected myself to during the summer of 2008 that has resulted in short-term memory loss. In other words, I really hope I have included everyone, as this book is my life's work thus far, and I want everyone who helped to know my heart-felt thanks.

First and foremost, I must thank Rob Caron and Sean Laberee for inspiring me to write tips about Visual Studio. Sean provided the vision, and Rob kept me going.

Since this is my first book, I never understood why nearly every author in their acknowledgements section profusely thanks their book publishers and editors. Now I completely understand. Thanks to Ben Ryan, Devon Musgrave, and Melissa von Tschudi-Sutton at Microsoft Press for their excellent guidance in my first publication, their patience with all my newbie questions, and their ability to set my expectations about how much effort goes into capturing screen shots. Thanks again for this opportunity to help my hometown. Also, I need to give a shout out to Jim Newkirk for all the book-writing advice that kept me, the deer in headlights, from dying of pure fright.

To my peer reviewers, who despite their own demanding work schedules, made the time to review my chapters and give me detailed feedback on such a short notice, I could not have put together this book without you. My heart-felt thanks to Dylan Lingelbach, Sean Laberee, Fiona Fung, Chris McGuire, Josh Stevens, Noah Coad, Habib Heydarian, Monica Boris, Douglas Hodges, Pat Brenner, Rahul Jajoo, and Rob Caron.

I have to acknowledge those who kept my head above water during the summer of 2008. Thanks to Charlie Calvert for the support and the confidence boosts as we prepared to speak at TechEd on the Visual Studio IDE tips and tricks. Thanks to Bryan Kirschner for the encouragement and the support for my talk at the O'Reilly's Open Source Convention, as I faced many chapter deadlines during that time. And my heart-felt thanks to everyone on the CodePlex team for sharing an office with me this entire time.

Lastly, thanks to my parents Jane and Louie Smolensky, for introducing me to computers at such a young age and an endless supply of Legos.

Chapter 1
Get Back to Basics with Your Editor

Performance improvements in Microsoft Visual Studio begin in the editor. There's no other action you do more than just pure typing, whether you are typing code, editing code, or deleting code. Think of these tips as a coin jar, where you put your spare change. Even if one of these tips saves you a few seconds, those few seconds really start to add up throughout the days, weeks, and months. That's a lot of spare time saved!

Basic Editing

Regardless of whether you're coding in C# or editing a plain text file, there are some basic tips you can use for any editing experience.

Text Editing

Over time, we developers form "muscle memory" for how to perform certain tasks, and we do a task in this familiar way even if there's a more efficient way. For example, consider deleting the current line of text in a file. Your first instinct might be to press Home, then Shift+End, and then Delete. Obviously, this sequence works just fine, and thanks to muscle memory, you'll never even consider looking up the corresponding keyboard shortcut. But imagine the second or two (or more if you hit the wrong key by accident) you would save if you could press just two keys to perform the same action. Although the amount of time you'll save might seem small at that moment, consider how the savings can add up if you are constantly deleting lines of text.

Tip 1.1: How to not accidentally copy a blank line

> **Sara Aside** There's something about me that wants to hit Ctrl+C instead of Ctrl+V whenever I'm on a blank line. I just don't understand it. So what happens is I copy a blank line, erasing the text I was trying to paste right there. And to my dismay, I hit Ctrl+V and nothing happens. In fact, I sometimes realize that I've accidentally hit Ctrl+C, so I hit Ctrl+V as fast as I can, thinking I can outrun the editor. But I lose every time.

The option that saved my sanity is found in Tools–Options–Text Editor–All Languages–General. There's a check box called Apply Cut Or Copy Commands To Blank Lines When There Is No Selection. Unchecking this option allows me to press Ctrl+C all I want on a blank line without losing the content on my clipboard.

☐ Apply Cut or Copy commands to blank lines when there is no selection

Tip 1.2: How to cycle through the Clipboard ring to paste different things

Sara Aside For me, this is yet another one of those moments where I exclaim, "Why can't I ever remember this tip?! It would save me so much time! Argh!" But then again, every time I'm reminded about this tip, it's like getting a little gift in the mail.

You can cycle through the past 20 items you've either cut or copied onto the Clipboard via Ctrl+Shift+V. Pretty cool, huh?

To illustrate, let's suppose you have two *Console.WriteLine()* calls and you need to swap the two strings, as shown in the following example:

```
class Program
{
    static void Main(string[] args)
    {
        Console.WriteLine("World");
        Console.WriteLine("Hello");
    }
}
```

Start by cutting both strings: "World" first, and "Hello" second. Now go to the first *Console. WriteLine()* call. When you press Ctrl+Shift+V once inside the parentheses, you'll get the following changes to the code:

```
class Program
{
    static void Main(string[] args)
    {
        Console.WriteLine("Hello");
        Console.WriteLine();
    }
}
```

Next, move to the second *Console.WriteLine()* call, and press Ctrl+Shift+V twice in a row. You'll get this:

```
class Program
{
    static void Main(string[] args)
    {
        Console.WriteLine("Hello");
        Console.WriteLine("World");
    }
}
```

And you store up to 20 items before the Clipboard cycles, meaning that it'll go back to the first item still recorded on the Clipboard. This is why the feature is called a Clipboard *ring*.

Tip 1.3: You can use Ctrl+Enter to insert a line above and Ctrl+Shift+Enter to insert a line below

In the following example, note the location of the cursor in the middle of the current line. Pressing Ctrl+Enter inserts a blank line above the current line, and Ctrl+Shift+Enter inserts a blank line below the current line. The cursor moves to the beginning of the new line.

```
·static·void·Main(string[]·args)
·{
·····//·Press·Ctrl+Enter·to·insert·blank·line·above

·····Console.WriteLine("Hello·World");

·····//·Press·Ctrl+Shift+Enter·to·insert·blank·line·below
·}
```

Tip 1.4: You can use Ctrl+W to select the current word

Press Ctrl+W at any location on a word to select the entire word. You can have the cursor at the end of word and still have it select the current word (instead of the proceeding white space).

```
·Sub·Main()
·····'·Ctrl+W·selects·current·word
·····Dim·i·As·Integer·=·1
·····i·+=·1
·End·Sub
```

If the cursor is in the middle of some white space, defined as two or more spaces, the white space will be selected.

Tip 1.5: You can use Ctrl+Delete to delete the next word and Ctrl+Backspace to delete the preceding word

> **Sara Aside**   Many of my "Tip of the Day" ideas come from looking through my old test cases. The Ctrl+Delete test case caught my eye because I had completely forgotten about this keyboard shortcut!

Ctrl+Delete deletes the next word the editor finds. The command is *Edit.WordDeleteToEnd*.

Ctrl+Backspace deletes the previous word. The command is *Edit.WordDeleteToStart*.

```
·Sub·Main()
·····'·Delete·WriteLine·by·pressing·Ctrl+Delete
·····Console.WriteLine("Hello·World")
·End·Sub
```

Tip 1.6: You can use Ctrl+L to cut the current line and Ctrl+Shift+L to delete the current line

Ctrl+L cuts the current line, including the end-of-line character (EOL). The command is *Edit.LineCut.*

Ctrl+Shift+L deletes the current line, including the EOL. The command is *Edit.LineDelete.*

Here's an example of Ctrl+L being used. In this example, you'll see the cursor before the *Console.WriteLine()* call.

```
·Sub·Main()
·····'·Press·Ctrl+L·to·cut·current·line
·····Console.WriteLine("Hello·World")
·End·Sub
```

And after you hit Ctrl+L, the line disappears.

```
·Sub·Main()
·····'·Press·Ctrl+L·to·cut·current·line
·End·Sub
```

But let's continue on with a bonus tip . . . Shift+Delete cuts the current line, including the EOL, if nothing is selected on the current line. If text is selected, Shift+Delete cuts just that text.

Tip 1.7: How to delete horizontal white space at the beginning of a line

> **Sara Aside** I always thought that "white space" was one word, but according to the Visual Studio UI, it is apparently two words. For this tip, I'll let the UI win and call it "white space."

On the Edit–Advanced menu, you'll find the Delete Horizontal White Space command bound to Ctrl+K, Ctrl+\.

Delete Horizontal White Space	Ctrl+K, Ctrl+\

To use, put the cursor anywhere in the white space that precedes the line and press Ctrl+K, Ctrl+\. You can also select multiple lines and delete the white space at the beginning of each line.

```
        ........static·void·Main(string[]·args)
        .........{
Console.WriteLine("Hello World");
Console.Read();
    ........}
```

Tip 1.8: You can drag code or text to a new location

Sara Aside   I tend to be more of a keyboard user, probably because I'm too lazy to reach all that way for the mouse. When I first saw this functionality, I was surprised because it is just not something I would intuitively think of, but of course it makes complete sense once the "Oh, I haven't seen that before" feeling wears off.

Select the code block you want to move by holding down the primary mouse button, and then *drag* the mouse pointer to the desired location. To copy code to the new location, hold down the Ctrl key.

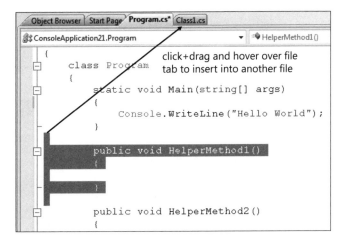

Not impressed? You can also drag code to a different file. Drag the code above the desired file tab, as shown next.

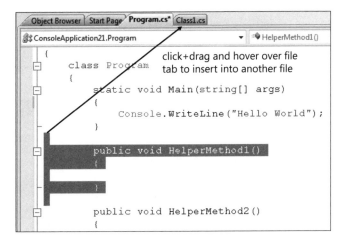

Although you'll get the mouse "can't drop" pointer, the editor will switch to that file. Then just move the mouse pointer down into the file, and you'll see the good ol' "drag and drop" pointer again. Enjoy!

Tip 1.9: You can right-drag code to Move Here or Copy Here

Sara Aside The idea for this tip was submitted by a blog reader. I had no clue that this menu item existed.

Select a line of code, and then right-drag that line to anywhere within your editor (or into another editor window). Then you'll get this little menu popup with the options of Move Here, Copy Here, and Cancel.

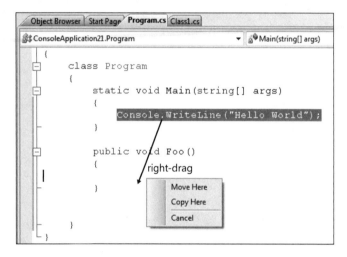

Sara Aside I love it when blog readers give me little tips like these, especially when I never knew they existed. This tip inspired me to start playing the game "Stump the Sara," where I asked blog readers to send me their most obscure IDE tricks. Since I only worked on the Visual Studio Core Team, the tips had to be limited to generic IDE features not tied to any specific language.

Tip 1.10: How to transpose characters, words, and lines in the editor

You can use three commands for transposing or swapping text in the editor, namely:

- Press Ctrl+T to transpose a character.
- Press Ctrl+Shift+T to transpose a word.
- Press Alt+Shift+T to transpose a line.

In the following example (where the cursor is placed before the "is" on the commented line "now is the time"), I'll apply the three commands to illustrate how text is swapped.

```
·static·void·Main(string[]·args)
·{
·····//·now·is·the·time
·····Console.WriteLine("Hello·World");
·····Console.Read();
·}
```

- Pressing Ctrl+T swaps "i" and the previous space, creating "// nowi s the time".

- Pressing Ctrl+Shift+T swaps "is" and "the", creating "// now the is time".

- Pressing Alt+Shift+T swaps the current line with the line below it.

Tip 1.11: You can use a keyboard shortcut to uppercase or lowercase a word in the editor

Once again, this tip illustrates that you can save time by using a keyboard shortcut versus having to type out your changes manually.

- Press Ctrl+Shift+U to make the current character or selected characters uppercase.

- Press Ctrl+U to make the current character or selected characters lowercase.

> **Sara Aside** I have to be honest here and say I had to ask around the Visual Studio building to find out under what conditions these commands would be useful. One scenario is where the Caps Lock key is bound to be a control key. For example, you type a word, then press Ctrl+Shift+Left Arrow to select, then use Ctrl+Shift+U to uppercase (instead of having to hold the Shift key down to type the entire word). Or maybe IntelliSense has made me lazy. =D

Undo/Redo

In the text editor toolbar, you'll find the Undo and Redo buttons. But if you look closely, you'll see a drop-down arrow, meaning that these buttons are actually drop-down controls, displaying your last undo and redo actions.

Tip 1.12: How to use the Undo stack on the standard toolbar

Instead of having to press Ctrl+Z or Ctrl+Y multiple times to undo or redo multiple commands, you can drop down the Undo or Redo button and, starting from the last action, select how many consecutive additional actions you want to undo or redo.

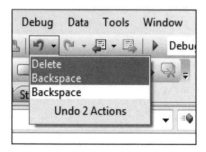

Just make sure the cursor is in a text editor to enable these buttons.

Scrolling and Navigation

Being able to view your code and move your cursor to whatever line catches your eye is just as important as being able to type your code as effortlessly as possible.

Scrolling

We've all used the mouse wheel to scroll code and text within the editor. The following tips introduce a few new keyboard shortcuts to improve your scrolling experience. Also, you may want to know how to hide the scrollbars altogether. Hey, you never know when those few extra pixels will come in handy.

Tip 1.13: How to use the mouse wheel for scrolling in all directions

Did you know that you can press down on the mouse wheel and have it act as a third button? For many applications that have an editor, pressing the mouse wheel displays an icon indicating which directions you can scroll in. Some require holding down the mouse wheel; others don't.

In the editor, press the mouse wheel just once and you'll see an icon indicating which directions you can scroll in.

```
·Sub·HelperFunction1()
·····Console.WriteLine
·End·Sub
```

A couple of things to note:

- The farther away the mouse is from the directional icon, the faster the editor will scroll.

- Pressing the primary mouse button stops the scroll, but you have to press the button again to move the cursor to the desired location.

Tip 1.14: How to jump to the top or bottom of the current view in the editor without scrolling

Unlike pressing PgUp or PgDn, which causes the editor to move either up or down a page, the following keyboard shortcuts cause only the cursor to move:

- Ctrl+PgUp jumps the cursor to the top of the current editor view without moving the current view, unlike a PgUp.

```
········protected·Node·head;
········protected·Node·current·=·
········//·Nested·type·is·also·ge
```

- Ctrl+PgDn jumps the cursor to the bottom of the current editor view without moving the current view, unlike a PgDn.

```
··············get·{·return·next.
··············set·{·next·=·value
```

If you find yourself using the keyboard shortcuts just shown, you may find these additional shortcuts helpful:

- Ctrl+Shift+PgUp selects all the text between the current cursor location (near the bottom of the screen in the following illustration) and the top of the current editor view.

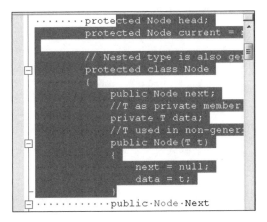

■ Ctrl+Shift+PgDn selects all the text between the current cursor location and the bottom of the current editor view.

One thing to note is that all four commands jump the cursor straight up, meaning that it doesn't go to the beginning of the line on that top line, but rather it goes as close as possible to the current column position, as you saw in the preceding illustrations.

Tip 1.15: You can hide the vertical and horizontal scroll bars in the editor

This tip truly embraces the spirit of "Did you know?"

Go to Tools–Options–Text Editor–General, and under Display, you can uncheck the Vertical Scroll Bar and the Horizontal Scroll Bar options.

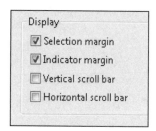

Now your scroll bars are hiding from you. And yes, you can still scroll both vertically and horizontally in this state.

```
Generics.cs                          ▼ ✕
Generics_CSharp.MyList ▼   ⇕ MyList()                ▼
      ··protected·Node·head;
      ··protected·Node·current·=·nul
      ··//·Nested·type·is·also·gener
  □ ··protected·class·Node
    ··{
      ······public·Node·next;
      ······//T·as·private·member·da
      ······private·T·data;
      ······//T·used·in·non-generic·
  □ ······public·Node(T·t)
      ······{
      ·········next·=·null;
      ·········data·=·t;
  ┕ ······}
  □ ······public·Node·Next
      ······{
      ·········get·{·return·next;·}
      ·········set·{·next·=·value;·
  ┕ ······}
```

Navigating Within and Among Editors

Navigating code is another activity you do so frequently that any time you save greatly adds up in the long run. The next tips get you to where you want to be, or back to where you just were, as fast as possible.

Tip 1.16: How to navigate forward and backward in the editor all because of go-back markers

In the standard toolbar, there are Navigate Backward and Navigate Forward icons.

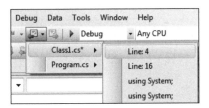

In the editor, the Navigate Backward command is bound to Ctrl+Minus, and the Navigate Forward command is bound to Ctrl+Shift+Minus. I find these commands most helpful when navigating around multiple files or jumping through call stacks.

This concludes your "Basic Editor Navigation 101" course. Now it is time for the "Advanced Editor Navigation 201" course.

You may have noticed that the Navigate Backward button additionally contains a drop-down list box. Displaying the items in this list box shows you all the places that have a go-back marker. In other words, when you hit the Navigate Backward button, you are going to the most recently visited go-back marker.

If we've done our jobs right, the go-back navigation should feel natural. But if you're like me, you like to know the little ins and outs of how things work.

A go-back marker is dropped under the following conditions:

- An incremental search (including reverse) leaves a go-back marker at the beginning of the search and another one at the end.

- A Go To Line action, like Ctrl+G, or a mouse-click that moves the cursor 11 lines or more from the current position drops a go-back marker at the new location.

- A destructive action (like hitting Backspace) after having moved the cursor to a new location drops a go-back marker.

- Doing a search, like Ctrl+F, drops a go-back marker at the found location.

- Opening a file drops a go-back marker wherever the cursor was on the old file and drops another on the opened file.

If you've found a condition where you'd like to see a go-back marker dropped, let me know.

Tip 1.17: How to use Undo to jump the cursor back to the last insertion point

In Tip 1.16, you learned more than you ever wanted to know about go-back markers. For this tip, you'll learn how insertion points are slightly different. They are similar to the go-back markers, but they are applied anywhere you click the mouse or jump the cursor to. The go-back marker "11 or more lines" rule doesn't apply.

The option, which is shown in the next illustration, can be found at Tools–Options–Text Editor–General.

☑ Include insertion point movements in Undo list

To give it a try, just click somewhere, then click somewhere else (or use Find or a Go To Line if you're using the keyboard), and then click Undo. You'll move back to that previous location.

Tip 1.18: How to reach the navigation bar via the keyboard

At the very top of the editor and just below the file tab channel, you'll find the navigation bar. The left combo box lists objects, and the right one lists the selected object's members. These combo boxes are very useful when you need to jump to various functions throughout a large solution or you want to see what functions an object has.

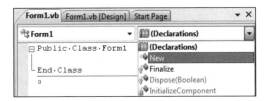

To jump to the navigation bar via the keyboard, press Ctrl+F2. This keyboard shortcut is bound to the *Window.MoveToNavigationBar* command. To toggle between the Objects list and the Members list, press Tab or Shift+Tab.

Additionally, you can hide (or show) the navigation bar by going to Tools–Options–Text Editor–All Languages–General and setting the Navigation Bar option to the desired setting. Note that since this option is found in the All Languages pane, you can customize it for any listed language under the Text Editor node.

Tip 1.19: How to split a window and create new windows

There are two ways to split the current window:

- From the Menu Bar, go to Window–Split.

- Using the mouse, grab the splitter control found directly above the document scrollbar, as shown in the next illustration.

But the split command works only horizontally. If you need to split vertically as illustrated in the following picture, use the *Window.NewWindow* command found at Window–New Window. This will create the windows "Program.cs:1" and "Program.cs:2." Then you can use the Window–New Vertical Tab Group command to separate both files with a vertical divider.

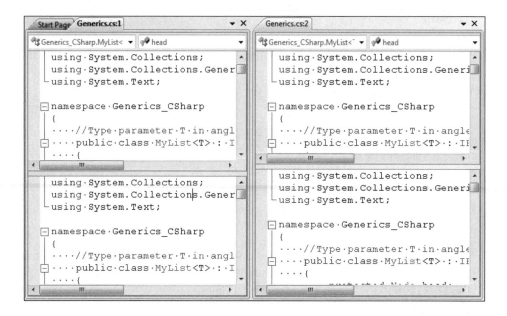

Tip 1.20: You can use F6 to jump between split panes in the editor

Sara Aside When I originally wrote and published this tip, I had to laugh at the fact that there was a six-month gap between this tip and Tip 1.19, which describes how to split the panes. The first week I started the "Tip of the Day" series on my blog, I came to the harsh reality that you actually have to write a tip of the day *every single day*. I was at a conference during the first week of writing "Tip of the Day," so the initial tips were those I could write the fastest. There was no rhyme or reason behind the madness; hence, the six-month gap between Tip 1.19 and Tip 1.20.

Once you have used the splitter to split the editor window, you can use F6 to jump between the editor views.

```
namespace·Generics_CSharp
{
·····//Type·parameter·T·in·angle·brackets.
·····public·class·MyList<T>·:·IEnumerable<T>
·····{
```

```
using·System.Collections;
using·System.Collections.Generic;
using·System.Text;
```

```
namespace·Generics_CSharp
{
```

Tip 1.21: How to enable URL navigation within the editor

Under Tools–Options–Text Editor–All Languages–General, there is the Enable Single-Click URL Navigation option. This option is enabled by default for most editors. But, just in case you're not able to click on a URL, here's where to go to verify the option is set.

Tip 1.22: How to use Ctrl+G without the Go To Line dialog box popping up

This tip is pretty straightforward: Pressing Ctrl+G will pop up the Go To Line dialog box.

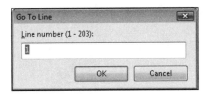

But did you know there's a way to use Ctrl+G without bringing up this dialog box?

1. Press Ctrl+D to go to the Find combo box on the standard toolbar.

2. Type in the line number.

3. Press Ctrl+G. (Note: Do *not* press Enter; if you do, you'll search for the number!)

Congrats! You've just navigated to the line without the Go To Line window coming up.

You can try to navigate to line 0, but Visual Studio will take you to line 1.

Word Wrap versus Virtual Space

The word wrap option wraps a long line of text, displaying on a new line the text that doesn't fit on the first line. The virtual space option allows you to have an insertion point anywhere on the file, even beyond the end-of-line character.

Tip 1.23: How to enable word wrap

The next image illustrates wrapping a line of text onto the next line.

```
              static void Main(string[]  ₽
⊟args)
          {
|               Console.WriteLine(      ₽
 "Hello World");
                Console.Read();
          }
```

Go to Tools–Options–Text Editor–All Languages–General, and check the Word Wrap option. When it is checked, you'll also have the option to Show Visual Glyphs For Word Wrap.

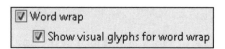

You can customize the foreground color of the visual glyph for a word wrap on the Tools–Options–Environment–Fonts And Colors by modifying the Visible White Space item.

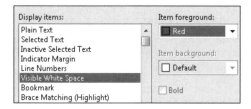

Tip 1.24: How to enable virtual space

> **Sara Aside** This tip is mutually exclusive to the previously mentioned word wrap feature, Tip 1.23. Try as you might, you won't be able to enable both word wrap and virtual space. But if you figure out a way to do it, please don't hesitate to let me know how you did it!

In the following example, the cursor is located in the virtual space. I have enabled the Visible White Space option to illustrate there are no spaces after the *Program* class name.

```
namespace ConsoleApplication21
{
    class Program
    {
        static void Main(string[] args)
        {
            Console.WriteLine("Hello World");
            Console.Read();
        }
    }
}
```

> **Sara Aside** I never use word wrap, and I made it through only a few weeks using virtual space when I was testing it. Neither option was quite for me. When I posted this tip, I asked readers to describe why they use these options. I knew I would learn something new.

Editor Fonts and Colors

This section focuses on how you can tweak anything in your editor that has some visual element to it, whether you just want to increase your text editor font sizes or display line numbers.

Font Size

It is fairly well known that you can go to Tools–Options–Environment–Fonts And Colors and select Plain Text to increase the overall font size of text in the editor. But there are a couple of other options for increasing font size that might come in handy.

Tip 1.25: How to increase the editor's ToolTip font size

Go to Tools–Options–Environment–Fonts And Colors and, under Show Settings For, select Editor Tooltip.

Show settings for:

| Editor Tooltip | ▼ | Use Defaults |

Font (bold type indicates fixed-width fonts):   Size:

| Verdana | ▼ | | 12 | ▼ |

Then you can customize the font and font size.

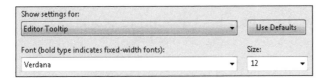

```
using System;
using namespace System ns.Generic;
using System.Text;
```

Tip 1.26: You can bind macros to keyboard shortcuts (or, "How to quickly increase or decrease your text editor font size")

> **Sara Aside**   I wrote the accessibility macros, which were my 133-line contribution to the Visual Studio 2005 product. You'll also find them in Visual Studio 2008.

Go to Tools–Options–Environment–Keyboard and, in the Show Settings For edit box, type **macro**. You'll see a list of samples at the top.

There are two accessibility macros worth noting: the increase and decrease text editor font size macros.

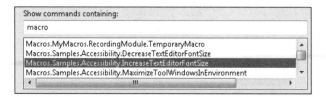

If you are using the General Development Settings and do not want to cause any conflicts with other keyboard shortcuts, bind the increase macro to Ctrl+Alt+Shift+UpArrow and the decrease macro to Ctrl+Alt+Shift+DownArrow. Of course, you can bind them to whatever shortcut you want, but these will not conflict with General Development Settings.

Now open the editor and try out the keyboard shortcuts. Remember that you have to hold down the Ctrl+Alt+Shift keys and press the up or down arrow repeatedly to really experience the full effect. Enjoy!

Fonts and Colors

Beyond just changing font sizes, you probably have wanted to change font colors. These next tips walk you through the various options available.

Tip 1.27: How to change the editor background to black

It's all about the simple things in life.

Go to Tools–Options–Environment–Fonts And Colors and, in Display Items, select Plain Text. Now set Item Foreground to White and Item Background to Black. And enjoy!

```
using System;
using System.Collections.Generic;
using System.Text;

namespace ConsoleApplication21
{
```

In the preceding screen shot, I set Keywords to Cyan to make the picture look pretty. (Of course, you can't see this change in this black-and-white book.)

Tip 1.28: What's the difference between Automatic and Default in Tools–Options–Environment–Fonts And Colors?

> **Sara Aside** Of all the pieces of UI in Visual Studio, I think these two options confuse me the most. I keep forgetting what the difference is, but at least now I have them written down for the rest of time.

I'm referring to the two settings, Automatic and Default, that appear in the colors drop-down list in Fonts And Colors.

Hold on tight, because here we go with my attempt at an explanation....

Automatic means that the color is inherited from some other element. For example, consider the Foreground Color for the Display Item: Visible White Space. Automatic is black, whereas Default is blue. *Automatic* in this context is inherited from the operating system's Window Text.

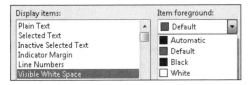

To change the operating system's Window Text on a computer running Windows Vista, go to Control Panel\Appearance and Personalization\Personalization–Window Color And Appearance–Open Classic Appearance Properties For More Color Options, and click the Advanced button. Then select Window to change Window Text Foreground and Background, Color and Color 1 respectively.

To illustrate the point about it being inherited from some other element, I've set Window Text to use a little green, setting the foreground color to bright green and the background color to dark green. For example, the text "Window Text" is in bright green and the background is in dark green.

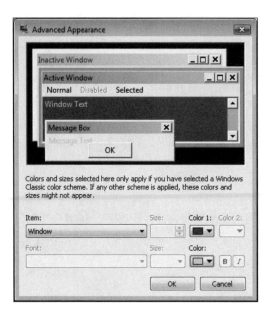

Let's look at Visible White Space again. Automatic is bright green (coming from the Window Text setting), and Default is still blue. If you are wondering why everything else is green, I'll explain that shortly, but first, let's take it one step at a time.

Default is what Visual Studio says the default is, which may depend on your .vssettings file you selected at first launch (for example, in the General Development Settings) or the last .vssettings file you reset to via the Tools–Import And Export Settings. You can also use the Use Default button on the Tools–Options–Environment–Fonts And Colors page to do this quick reset.

For my configuration and probably for all the .vssettings files, Visible White Space has a default color of blue. It's up to you whether you want to have it come from the operating system's Window Text or from what Visual Studio says the best default color is.

Okay, cool. But why did so many other elements change colors?

Plain Text is interesting because its Default is set to Automatic. This is why whenever you try to set it to Automatic, it shows Default the next time you bring up the UI. In other words, think of Plain Text as always coming from the operating system's Window Text. And since we set Plain Text to Green, every UI element in the IDE that derives its colors from Plain Text turned to green.

> **Sara Aside** Finally, this is written down. So I can now forget it again. =D

Tip 1.29: How to change a bookmark color

I call out the bookmark color since it appears at the top of the Fonts And Colors Display Items list. But this tip applies to all items that appear in the indicator margin, like current statement, breakpoints, and so on. But let's focus on bookmarks for this tip.

This picture shows a bookmark icon/glyph in the indicator margin:

So let's change the color to red! Go to Tools–Options–Environment–Fonts And Colors. Under Display Items, select Bookmark. Now change the background color to something else, like red. You'll notice that *nothing* changes in the editor.

To have a different bookmark color, you need to remove the indicator margin. Go to Tools–Options–Text Editor–General and uncheck Indicator Margin. Now you'll see the bookmark appear in red.

The indicator margin just shows icons (or glyphs, to be more accurate), which are not customizable. This is why you're only able to change the foreground color and why you may not see the change. I guess a better title for this tip is "Why didn't the bookmark color change?" I hope this helps clarify any confusion.

Visual Cues

Some of the following tips are enabled by default whereas others you might have a hard time trying to find, like viewing visible white space.

Tip 1.30: How to track changes in the editor

The tracking changes feature provides the following visual aids to let you know where your last saved and unsaved edits are:

- **Yellow**   You've edited these lines since your last save. Yellow becomes green upon saving.

- **Green**   These are the lines you edited before your last save. Save again and green disappears.

Not seeing it? Go to the Tools–Options dialog box and, on the Text Editor–General page, check the Track Changes check box. And now you know how to turn it off.

Still not seeing it? Make sure the Text Editor–General page has the Selection Margin check box checked.

Tip 1.31: How to show line numbers in the editor

Go to Tools–Options–Text Editor–All Languages–General, and check Line Numbers to show line numbers for all files.

If you just want to see (or not see) the line numbers of a specific file, you can override this global setting by going to the Text Editor–*<specific language>*–General page.

Tip 1.32: How to view visible white Space

> **Sara Aside**   Here is a simple, but very powerful, little feature, especially when you deal with white space as much as I did when I tested the editor. The first time I saw one of our developers using it, I thought, "Yuck!" But now I can't live without it.

There are two ways to enable this feature:

- From the menu bar, go to Edit–Advanced–View White Space.

- From the keyboard, press Ctrl+R, Ctrl+W.

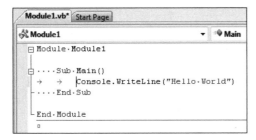

Note that this command is available only when a file is open. Even though this command is shown only in the menu, the visible white space setting persists for all files and all Visual Studio launches.

Printing

It was a bittersweet day when I learned that you can print to a file, using the Microsoft XPS Document Writer that appears in the list of installed printers in the Print dialog box. It was sweet because it made testing printing so much faster. But it was bitter because all my grand plans of buying a top-of-the-line color printer for my office became moot.

Printing Options

We all have to print at some point. So, when the time comes for you to print a file, it's good to know what your options are in customizing how your printed pages look.

Tip 1.33: How to print line numbers

> **Sara Aside** Back in the Visual Studio .NET 2003 days, you had to go to File–Page Setup and check Line Numbers (in the lower left corner) to print line numbers, regardless of whether they were visible in the editor. For Visual Studio 2005 and beyond, we moved this option to the Print dialog box.

To print line numbers, go to File–Print, and on the lower left, you'll see two options:

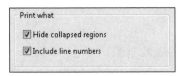

Here's a bonus tip, because I cannot bring myself to write a "Did you know … how to hide collapsed regions when printing" tip. It makes me yawn. You can also hide collapsed regions. I've used this when I wanted to print out just my test case function and I didn't want to print out any of the helper functions because they all lived in the same test case file.

```
 1 Public Class Class1
 2     Public Sub Test()
 3         HelperMethod1()
 4         HelperMethod2()
 5     End Sub
 6
 7     Private Sub HelperMethod1 ...
10
11     Private Sub HelperMethod2 ...
14 End Class
15
```

The preceding illustration, which I printed to an .xps file (no, I didn't scan in a printed page), shows how the hidden collapsed regions will print out as ellipses.

Tip 1.34: How to print boldly

I think we all, at one point in time, have tried to customize our editor colors or change keywords to bold or something else, and then pressed the Print button. Yet, we arrive at the printer confused that our changes haven't been applied.

To customize your fonts and colors for printing, go to Tools–Options–Environment–Fonts And Colors and change the selection in the Show Settings For drop-down list to Printer. Now you can customize your fonts and colors, including bold.

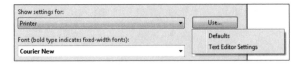

Additionally, let's say that you've already tweaked your colors or just want to use what you see in the editor. Then press the Use button and select Text Editor Settings. The default settings are restored to the original text editor defaults.

Tip 1.35: How to print the file path as the page header

Go to File–Page Setup. In the lower left corner, there's a Page Header option:

This option puts the file path across the top of the printed file.

```
                C:\Users\saraf\Desktop\Class1.vb
   1 Public Class Class1
   2       Public Sub Test()
   3            HelperMethod1()
   4            HelperMethod2()
   5       End Sub
   6
   7       Private Sub HelperMethod1 ...
  10
  11       Private Sub HelperMethod2 ...
  14 End Class
  15
```

Status Bar

The status bar gives you updates about what's going on in the IDE, whether you are doing a build, conducting a search, running a macro, or performing any other such operation.

Small features like the status bar always present a challenge, if not a dare, to a tester. Features like these nearly mock us with their "You'll never be able to find a new bug against me" attitude. Or maybe I'm just bitter that I don't recall finding any good bugs against the status bar.

Status Bar Options

As you would expect, there are not many options with the status bar. In fact, I believe this option might be the only one.

Tip 1.36: You can hide the status bar

I'm not sure why you may want to hide the status bar. Maybe when you are in Full Screen mode, you want those extra few pixels at the bottom for a true full-screen experience.

Whatever the reason, you can go to Tools–Options–Environment–General and uncheck Show Status Bar. Now Visual Studio does not have a status bar.

And while we're on the subject of the status bar, here's another quick tip to keep in mind if you choose to leave the status bar showing. You can double-click the section of the status bar that shows the line, column, and character to pop up the Go To Line dialog box.

Chapter 2
Make Your Editor Work for You

Throughout this book, you'll watch me go back and forth on what was my favorite feature to test. But I can say without a doubt that there was no other feature I wanted to get my hands on more badly than the editor. Hey, it is the one feature that *everyone uses all the time*. How could I not want to test it and break it?

Chapter 1, "Get Back to Basics with Your Editor," focuses on basic editing tips that can be applied for any file type—even a plain text file. This chapter focuses on basic coding tips for any language file. Here, you will find tips for Microsoft IntelliSense, outlining, and code snippets.

Advanced Editing

This section covers tips you should be aware of when coding. These tips present additional ways to select code, keyboard shortcuts for commenting code, quick mechanisms for formatting your code, and more!

Selection

There are numerous ways to select code beyond the standard mouse drag.

Tip 2.1: How to use box/column selection in the editor

The editor offers two different selection models: stream and box. There's also line selection, but that's only in Brief emulations. (See Tip 2.15 for more information on editor emulations.)

Stream selection, using Shift+Arrow key, is what everyone is familiar with. But box selection allows you to manually select columns and lines at the same time.

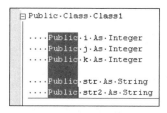

Just hold down Shift+Alt+Arrow key and you'll quickly get the feel for box selection. You can also use box selection using the mouse by holding down the Alt key while you select text. Cut, Copy, Paste still works, but just keep track of where you started to select the text. Ah, the memories of having to test all this functionality.

Tip 2.2: How to jump to the beginning of some selected text when hitting escape

I hope this tip's title makes sense. The idea is that you select some text and then hit Escape. Now where do you want the cursor to go?

If you want it to stay where it is, that's the default behavior. But if you want it to jump to the beginning of the selection (that is, the selection anchor), go to Tools–Options–Text Editor–General and check Go To Selection Anchor After Escape.

Tip 2.3: You can use Ctrl+= to select code from the current cursor location to the last go-back marker

See Tip 1.16 for more information about go-back markers.

The keyboard shortcut used to select code from the current cursor location to the last go-back marker is Ctrl+=, and the command is *Edit.SelectToLastGoBack*.

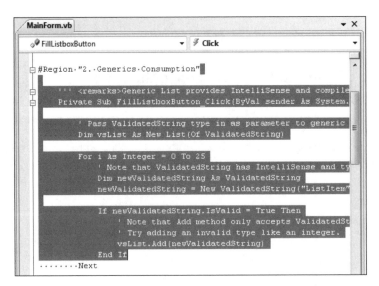

In the previous graphic, I started the cursor at the end of the #Region line and then clicked the mouse about 17 lines down to drop a go-back marker. Then I pressed Ctrl+= to select all the text back to the last go-back marker.

Tip 2.4: How to swap the current anchor position in the editor

Ctrl+K, Ctrl+A will swap the current anchor position.

> **Sara Aside**   To test Emacs emulations, I decided to write all my test cases in Emacs mode. (Emacs is a text editor, similar to Visual Studio. For details, see the Wikipedia article *http://en.wikipedia.org/wiki/Emacs*.) What was interesting is that I seemed to swap the anchor position all the time (using the appropriate shortcuts in Emacs mode); yet whenever I wasn't in Emacs mode, I never did this. I think it was just the way I was trained in college to think about the Emacs editing experience that made me want to swap the anchor position.

Cursor position before swap:

```
□ Module·Module1
│
□ ····Sub·Main()
│   ········Console.WriteLine("Hello")
│           Console.WriteLine("World")
└ ····End·Sub
```

Cursor position after swap:

```
□ Module·Module1
│
□ ····Sub·Main()
│   ········Console.WriteLine("Hello")
│           Console.WriteLine("World")
└ ····End·Sub
```

Commenting

Now that you know how to quickly select code, you can quickly comment or uncomment the selected lines through keyboard shortcuts.

Tip 2.5: How to quickly comment and uncomment code using keyboard shortcuts

Ah, it really is the simple things in life, isn't it?

Use Ctrl+K, Ctrl+C to comment code and Ctrl+K, Ctrl+U to uncomment code. All the default development settings have these commands bound to these keyboard shortcuts.

You can find these commands under the Edit–Advanced menu as shown here:

	Incremental Search	Ctrl+I
	Comment Selection	Ctrl+K, Ctrl+C
	Uncomment Selection	Ctrl+K, Ctrl+U

Formatting

You can have more control over your cut-and-paste scenarios, whether you are cutting code from a Web site and pasting it into your editor or pasting code into your favorite blog editor. This section presents numerous ways to quickly format your code as needed for a particular language.

Tip 2.6: You can display guidelines in the editor to help format your code

> **Sara Aside** The most popular tip on my blog is the one about guidelines. I think it is so popular because it was one of my very first tips about Microsoft Visual Studio many, many years ago. I've had a lot of people thank me for including that tip in my blog, but when a random developer stopped me in the hallway to thank me because he wrote the feature, that took hallway conversations to a new level. He had moved to another area of Visual Studio many years before my writing the tip, so he was very excited to see his feature get some public attention. I think one of the hardest things for any developer is to spend time coding a feature that never gets into the hands of a customer.

> **Important** To enable guidelines, you need to modify your registry settings. Please be aware that you use guidelines at your own risk and should do so only if you are comfortable modifying your registry settings. You will need to restart Visual Studio after modifying the registry for the changes to take affect.

Go to HKEY_CURRENT_USER\Software\Microsoft\VisualStudio\9.0\Text Editor.

Create a *String (RG_SZ)* key called Guides.

The value is in the format of *RBG(x,y,z) $n_1,...,n_{13}$*, where *x,y,z* are the RBG values and *n* is the column number. You can have at most 13 guidelines. For example, *RBG(255,0,0) 5,20* will put two red guidelines at column positions 5 and 20, as illustrated here:

```
using·System;
   using·System.Collections.Generic;
   using·System.Linq;
   using·System.Text;

namespace·ConsoleApplication23
   {
····class·Program
····{
········static·void·Main(string[]·args)
········{
············Console.WriteLine("Hello·World");
········}
····}
}
```

Tip 2.7: How to format the document, the selected text, or just the current line

Ever been typing in the editor and, for whatever reason, the text isn't indented properly on the line? Instead of manually pressing Backspace or Tab for each line of text, just press Ctrl+K, Ctrl+D, which performs the Format Document command.

For larger files, you might just want to select the region that isn't justified correctly and use Ctrl+K, Ctrl+F. This keyboard shortcut formats the current line if you have nothing selected.

These commands are found under the Edit–Advanced menu.

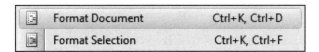

Tip 2.8: How to keep tabs or to insert spaces

> **Sara Aside** This tip and Tip 2.9 were my least favorite features to test. It drove me crazy trying to keep track of when a tab should get inserted, when the cursor should move to the correct formatted position, and so on and so forth. Now I use only spaces in my code. =)

Go to Tools–Options–Text Editor–<*Language*>–Tabs to switch between using tabs and inserting spaces.

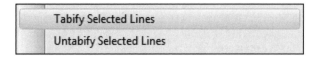

Note that you can set this for all languages on the Text Editor–All Languages page, but usually this is something you want to set for each individual language.

Tip 2.9: How to convert spaces to tabs and tabs to spaces

There are four commands that involve converting spaces to tabs and tabs to spaces. The first two commands are found on the Edit–Advanced menu:

- **Tabify Selected Lines**   Replaces the leading white space on a line that contains the selection with tabs.

- **Untabify Selected Lines**   Replaces the leading white space on a line that contains the selection with spaces.

Tabify Selected Lines
Untabify Selected Lines

 Note The Edit–Advanced–(Un)Tabify Selected Lines isn't supported for Microsoft Visual Basic.

The last two commands are not found on the Edit menu but are available for you to either bind to a keyboard shortcut or manually add to the Edit menu or Text Editor toolbar:

- *Edit.ConvertTabsToSpaces*   Converts selected white space to spaces.
- *Edit.ConvertSpacesToTabs*   Converts selected white space to tabs.

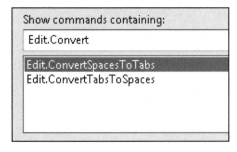

Note that you may have to uncheck Tools–Options–Text Editor–Basic–VB Specific–Pretty Listing (Reformatting) of Code to use *Edit.ConvertTabsToSpaces* and *Edit.ConvertSpacesToTabs*.

Tip 2.10: You can increase and decrease the line indent from the text editor toolbar

> **Sara Aside** Not one of my best "Tip of the Day" titles, but it illustrates the point. =)

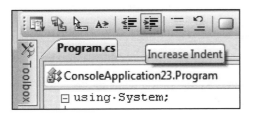

With either a single line or several lines selected, you can use either the Increase Indent or Decrease Indent command found on either the text editor toolbar or the Edit–Advanced menu (where it is listed as Increase/Decrease Line Indent).

Tip 2.11: What's the difference between smart indenting and block indenting?

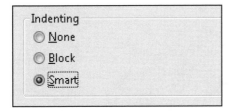

Smart indenting is the option you want, provided you want the cursor to be properly indented whenever you press Enter or the up and down arrows in the code. An example is when you create a new method called *Method1()* and then hit Enter. You'll notice the cursor automatically indents itself. If you continue to hit Enter, the cursor will remain indented. Not all languages support this smart indenting, but if the language you're using does, this should be the default setting for that language.

Block indenting is similar to a document editor. Using Visual Basic as an example, the difference here is when you type in *Method1()* and hit Enter, only that first new line is automatically indented. The next new line places the cursor at column 0.

Selecting None will not indent any new lines. You will have to indent everything manually.

Outlining

Take control of outlining, whether you want to quickly collapse or expand your code, or remove it altogether.

Tip 2.12: How to collapse and expand code

There are five commands for outline toggling; they can be found on the Edit–Outlining menu.

Toggle Outlining Expansion

```
Toggle Outlining Expansion    Ctrl+M, Ctrl+M
```

By pressing Ctrl+M, Ctrl+M anywhere within the code block, you can toggle between collapsing a given block of code (as shown here)

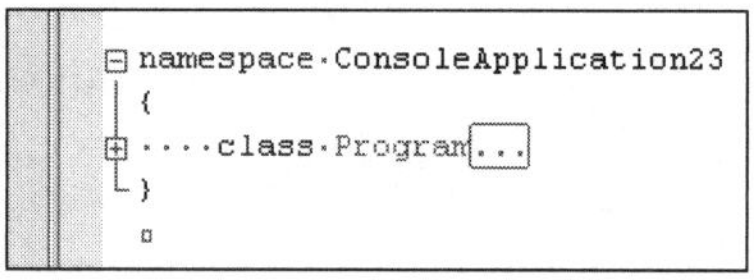

```
namespace ConsoleApplication23
{
    class Program...
}
```

and expanding it (as shown next)

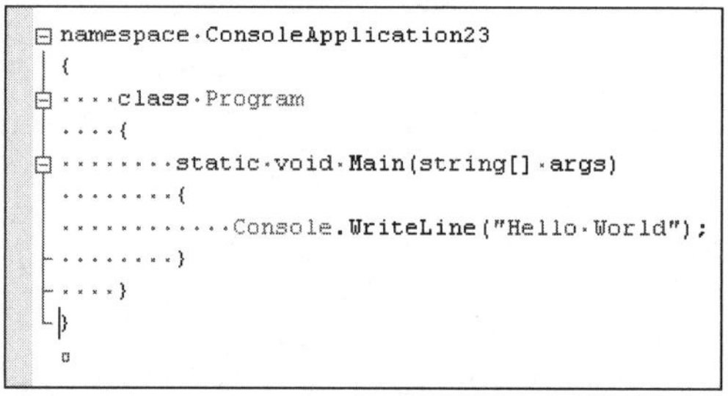

```
namespace ConsoleApplication23
{
    class Program
    {
        static void Main(string[] args)
        {
            Console.WriteLine("Hello World");
        }
    }
}
```

Toggle All Outlining

```
Toggle All Outlining          Ctrl+M, Ctrl+L
```

By pressing Ctrl+M, Ctrl+L anywhere in the editor, you can toggle between collapsing and expanding the entire file.

Completely collapsed:

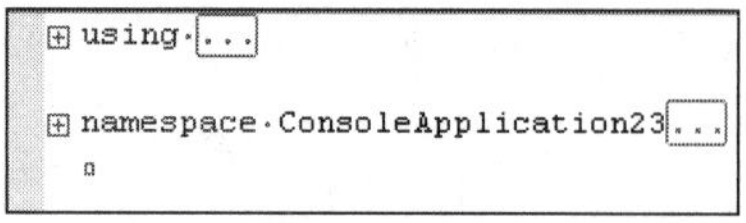

```
using ...

namespace ConsoleApplication23...
```

Completely expanded:

```
using·System;
  using·System.Collections.Generic;
  using·System.Linq;
  using·System.Text;

namespace·ConsoleApplication23
  {
  ····class·Program
  ····{
  ········static·void·Main(string[]·args)
  ········{
  ············Console.WriteLine("Hello·World");
  ········}

  ········static·string·HelperFunction()
  ········{
  ············return·"hello·world";
  ········}
  ····}
  }
  □
```

Stop Outlining

| Stop Outlining | Ctrl+M, Ctrl+P |

By pressing Ctrl+M, Ctrl+P anywhere in the editor, you can turn off outlining.

```
  namespace·ConsoleApplication23
  {
  ····class·Program
  ····{
  ········static·void·Main(string[]·args)
  ········{
  ············Console.WriteLine("Hello·World");
  ········}

  ········static·string·HelperFunction()
  ········{
  ············return·"hello·world";
  ········}
  ····}
  }
  □
```

Start Automatic Outlining

| Start Automatic Outlining |

Unfortunately, start outlining and stop outlining are not the same command, so you can't toggle between one state and the other. Additionally, using the General Development Settings, start outlining is not bound to a keyboard shortcut. So you need to go to Edit–Outlining–Start Automatic Outlining to turn on outlining again.

Collapse to Definitions

In my opinion, Collapse To Definitions is is the most useful of all the outlining commands (mostly because it was the only one I used, except for when I had to test the others). This command allows you to quickly glance at all of your functions.

```
namespace ConsoleApplication23
{
    class Program
    {
        static void Main(string[] args)...
        static string HelperFunction1()...
        static string HelperFunction2()...
    }
}
```

Tip 2.13: You can cut and paste a collapsed block of code

Sara Aside You can cut and paste a collapsed block of code, keeping all of the code inside intact. Of course, this is exactly what you would expect, but I never thought about trying it.

```
namespace ConsoleApplication23
{
    class Program
    {
        static void Main(string[] args)...
        static string HelperFunction2()...
        static string HelperFunction1()...
    }
}
```

With a block of code collapsed, as indicated to the right of the code lines shown in the preceding illustration, select the block and cut or just cut the line via your favorite mechanism for cutting a line. Now navigate to the desired location and paste.

```
namespace·ConsoleApplication23
{
····class·Program
····{
········static·void·Main(string[]·args) ...

········static·string·HelperFunction1() ...

········static·string·HelperFunction2()
········{
············return·"Helper·Function·2";
········}

····}
}
```

Note the code will be automatically expanded upon pasting.

The idea behind this tip is that you want to quickly cut and paste an entire function, but the function is quite long. You can use the approach shown in the previous tip (specifically, Ctrl+M, Ctrl+M to toggle between expanding and collapsing a block of code) to collapse the function to just the function name. Then press Ctrl+L to cut the current line. Now you can paste the function wherever you want.

Tip 2.14: You can hide outlining (selection margin) without turning off outlining

Go to Tools–Options–Text Editor–General, and uncheck Selection Margin. Although the left margin that indicates a code block is gone, outlining will still work.

```
namespace·ConsoleApplication23
{
····class·Program
····{
········static·void·Main(string[]·args) ...

········static·string·HelperFunction1() ...

········static·string·HelperFunction2() ...
····}
}
```

Emulations

Back in the day, during a summer research program at the University of Massachusetts, I was fortunate enough to use GNU Emacs every day all summer long. I use the word "fortunate" because five years later, I would be trying to "page-in" everything I learned about Emacs to test the Emacs editor emulations in Visual Studio.

The other emulation I tested was Brief. I didn't have any prior experience with Brief, so I was on my own to take a crash course. Fortunately, there was someone in the Visual Studio building who had used Brief, so I got to bounce a lot of ideas and questions off of him. However, this meant that I had to learn three different sets of keyboard shortcuts! I decided to cycle through the editor emulations, where one week I focused on Emacs, the next week I focused on Brief, and then I had a sanity-check week with the default editor. It was a very confusing time for my muscle memory.

But don't get me wrong, testing editor emulations was a tester's corner case heaven. Having been a program manager for a couple of years now, I completely understand what I put the developer and the program manager through by having them figure out what to do with all those bugs I found. But, it was still pure joy.

Tip 2.15: How to enable Emacs and Brief editor emulations

In Visual Studio 2005, we introduced Emacs and Brief emulations into the editor.

Go to Tools–Options–Environment–Keyboard, and then drop down the Apply The Following Additional Keyboard Mapping Scheme list. Then choose either Brief or Emacs.

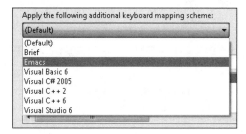

To return to the standard editor, just select (Default).

Binary Editor

You can use the binary editor to edit any resource, provided you want to edit it bit by bit. Yes, I came up with this bad joke all by myself.

Tip 2.16: How to open something in the binary editor

> **Sara Aside** The first time I saw this test case in the editor test bed, I thought, "Whoa, I've opened the Open File dialog box a thousand times and have never seen this option before."

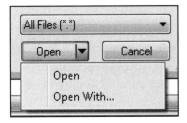

To use the binary editor, follow these steps:

1. Go to File–Open File.

2. Click the drop-down arrow on the Open button or, from the keyboard, just press the down arrow.

3. Choose Binary Editor and click OK or Open, depending on your Visual Studio version.

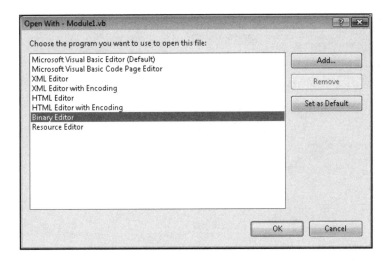

Delimiter Highlighting and Brace Matching

Ever needed a quick visual check to ensure you are lining up your code correctly? You can use the Automatic Delimiter Highlighting and Brace Matching features to give you that visual cue.

Tip 2.17: What does that Automatic Delimiter Highlighting option do?

Sara Aside Honestly, I had to ask around to find out what this one did. I simply couldn't remember.

☑ Automatic delimiter highlighting

Whenever you have code construct pairs (that's what the documentation calls them), when you finish typing either the start or end pair, both pairs of words become bold. To turn off this feature, go to Tools–Options–Text Editor–General and uncheck Automatic Delimiter Highlighting.

```
····class·Program
····{
········static·void·Main(string[]·args)
········{
#if·DEBUG
············Console.WriteLine("Hello·World");
#endif
········}
```

You can customize the color for the bolding by going to Tools–Options–Environment–Fonts And Colors and selecting Brace Matching (Highlight).

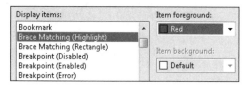

And now the #if and #endif appear in bold and in red.

```
····class·Program
····{
········static·void·Main(string[]·args)
········{
#if·DEBUG
············Console.WriteLine("Hello·World");
#endif
········}
```

Tip 2.18: How to change the Brace Matching color

You can change the Brace Matching color. Go to Tools–Options–Environment–Fonts And Colors, select Brace Matching (Rectangle), and set this option to the desired color.

And now your curly braces show up with a new highlight color.

```
····class·Program
····{
········static·void·Main(string[]·args)
········{
············Console.WriteLine("Hello·World");
········}|
```

> **Sara Aside** I like the bright green color. It must be Seattle's nine months of gray weather getting to me.

Clean up unused code

C# provides several interesting features for getting control back over your *using* statements.

Tip 2.19: You can remove unused *using* statements

In C#, there's the option to remove any of your unused *using* statements. This option is especially helpful if you're reusing some sort of template over and over again. Instead of having to comment out each line, compile, see whether the compile was successful, and then either remove or uncomment the line, you can bring up the editor context menu (just right-click in the editor) and choose Organize Usings–Remove Unused Usings. This will do all the hard work for you.

AutoRecover

Visual Studio provides an AutoRecover feature to keep you going in the case of an unexpected shutdown, power failure, or some other unfortunate event.

Tip 2.20: What does Visual Studio do to autorecover files in the case of an unexpected shutdown?

> **Sara Aside** People on the testing team used to tease the tester who owned the AutoRecover feature that every time there was a power failure in the building (because of a storm or other such event), he was standing near some big red switch in the off position with a grin on his face so that everyone in the building could test his features for him.

Under Tools–Options–Environment, you'll find the AutoRecover page.

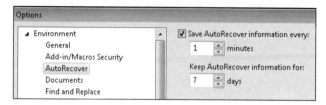

Note that you can opt out of the AutoRecover feature by unchecking the Save AutoRecover Information Every check box.

The rest of the page is self-explanatory, but did you know where Visual Studio saves these autorecovered files? They are saved in \My Documents\Visual Studio *<version>*\Backup Files*<projectname>*.

In case you (hopefully) have never seen the AutoRecover dialog box, here's what it looks like. It'll pop up the next time you launch Visual Studio after an unexpected shutdown. You have the options to either use the backup files or ignore them.

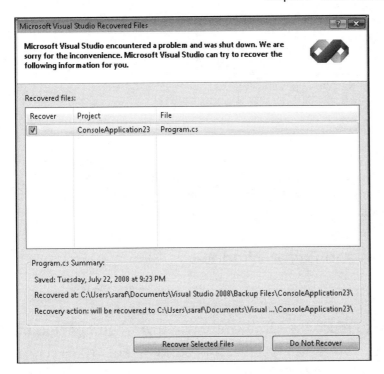

File Extensions

If you ever find yourself editing source code files that use a different file extension, it's good to know that you can still get syntax highlighting.

Tip 2.21: How to get syntax highlighting for a given file extension

On the Tools–Options–Text Editor–File Extension page, you can map a file extension to one of the included editors.

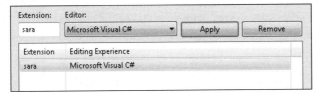

And after mapping the .sara extension to a C# editor, we now get syntax highlighting for the file.

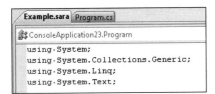

There is also an option to map files without extensions to a specific editor.

Opening Files

The more time you spend in the IDE, the more you'll want to customize your experience. The same is true for opening files. Since this is a frequent activity, you'll want shortcuts or some time-saving customizations to expedite getting your files opened where you want them.

Opening Files and Editor Windows

These next tips offer various customizations for opening a file in the editor.

Tip 2.22: How to reuse the same editor window when opening files

Go to Tools–Options–Environment–Documents, and check the Reuse Current Document Window, If Saved option to give this tip a try.

> ☑ Reuse current document window, if saved

If the current document window is dirty (meaning you've made a modification but haven't saved it yet), the next document opens in its own document window. However, if the current document is saved, the new document just opens over it.

I tried using this from time to time when I owned testing it, but it wasn't for me.

Tip 2.23: How to automatically refresh an open document in the editor

Under Tools–Options–Environment–Documents, there's the option to Detect When A File Is Changed Outside The Environment. Under it is the second option, to Autoload Changes, If Saved.

> **Sara Aside** I can't imagine working without having the first check box checked. However, as for the second one, I don't think I'm brave enough to enable it.

If only the first check box is checked, you'll get this prompt:

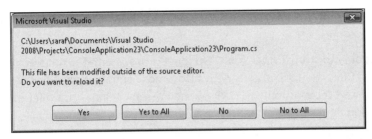

If you do a lot of modifying of files outside Visual Studio, I could see this dialog box getting annoying. But since the option is global and sticky across Visual Studio sessions, I wouldn't want to forget that I had it checked. But then again, this is coming from a very paranoid, risk-averse tester.

Tip 2.24: How to edit a read-only file in Visual Studio

In Tools–Options–Environment–Documents, there's the option Allow Editing Of Read-Only Files; Warn When Attempt To Save.

If this option is checked (my personal preference) and you attempt to save, you'll get prompted whether you want to overwrite the document or save it as something else. My thoughts are—if I'm editing the file, I want to overwrite it eventually.

If this option isn't checked and you attempt to edit the file, you'll get prompted whether to make the file writeable or perform an in-memory edit.

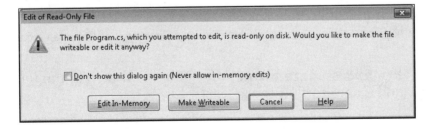

Tip 2.25: How to customize what directory the File–Open–File dialog box opens to

This tip is pretty straightforward. Under Tools–Options–Environment–Documents, there's the Open File Using Directory Of Currently Active Document option. When I first read this option, it took me a few seconds to think, "What's the open file thingy?" It's referring to the File–Open–File dialog box.

If you have this option checked, you'll open to the directory of the currently active document in the editor (the doc with the focus), as shown in the next image.

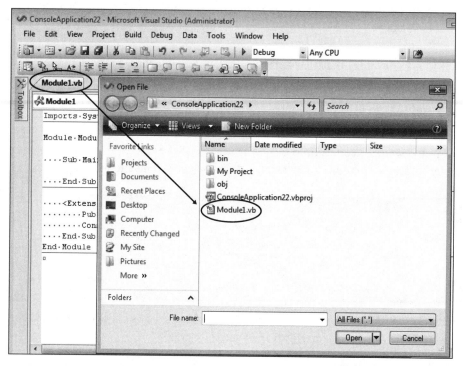

If you do not have this option checked, the File–Open–File dialog directory displays content as an MRU (most-recently used) list, opening to the last directory used to open a file.

Tip 2.26: How to customize the number of items shown in the Recent Files lists (and where to find those lists)

This tip explores the Recent Files options, found under Tools–Options–Environment–General.

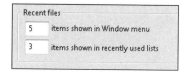

The Items Shown In Window Menu option controls the number of items to display in the Window menu. For example, if you set the option to 5, you will get only 5 items in the Window menu, as shown here:

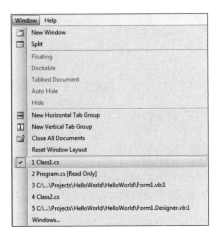

The Items Shown In Recently Used Lists controls the number of items found in the File–Recent Files and File–Recent Projects lists. When it is set to 3, you'll see only 3 files in these lists, as shown here:

Bookmarks

Bookmarks are a way for you to mark various locations in your files. When I first started testing bookmarks, I wasn't sure what the difference was between comments in the Task List and bookmarks. Task List comments and other tokens are found in the file, meaning that these have the potential of getting checked into your source code repository and being visible to everyone. On the other hand, bookmarks are for your eyes only. They are stored outside the file in the Bookmarks window. For more information on Task List features, see Chapter 5.

Managing Bookmarks

These next tips walk you through creating and using bookmarks.

Tip 2.27: How to set bookmarks and navigate among them

Press Ctrl+K, Ctrl+K to toggle a bookmark. The command is *Edit.ToggleBookmark*.

Press Ctrl+K, Ctrl+N to navigate to the next bookmark. The command is *Edit.NextBookmark*.

Press Ctrl+K, Ctrl+P to navigate to the previous bookmark. The command is *Edit. PreviousBookmark*.

You can also quickly get rid of all your bookmarks by pressing Ctrl+K, Ctrl+L. The command is *Edit.ClearBookmarks*.

All of these commands can be found under the Edit–Bookmarks menu and on the Text Editor toolbar. Note that on the Text Editor toolbar, the Previous Bookmark In Document and Next Bookmark In Document items don't have keyboard shortcuts bound to them, but they are listed on the Text Editor toolbar.

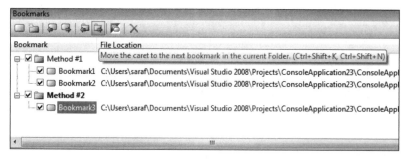

Tip 2.28: How to navigate among bookmark folders in the Bookmark window

There's a Bookmarks window that allows you to organize and arrange your bookmarks. You can create folders and store bookmarks within them.

Once you've organized your bookmarks, you can add the Shift key to the bookmark naviga-tion keyboard shortcuts to navigate within the folder:

- Use Ctrl+Shift+K, Ctrl+Shift+P to move to the previous bookmark in the folder.
- Use Ctrl+Shift+K, Ctrl+Shift+N to move to the next bookmark in the folder.

Tip 2.29: You can bookmark all of your Quick Find results

> **Sara Aside** It's funny—when I was writing this tip, I started looking all around the Find And Replace window trying to figure out where the option was to bookmark all of the results. Finally, it jumped right out at me. =)

If you hit Bookmark All instead of Find Next, bookmarks will be dropped at all the found locations.

And if you've accidentally bookmarked half of your code by searching for a frequently used search term (like I did the first time I tried this), simply open the Bookmarks window (View–Bookmarks Window), press Ctrl+A to select all bookmarks, and then hit Delete.

IntelliSense

The term *IntelliSense* refers to the editor functionality that offers suggestions to you as you type code. The major IntelliSense features that you are probably most familiar with are statement completion, parameter info, and complete word.

Statement Completion, Parameter Info, and Complete Word

Statement completion is the UI that displays what objects you can insert into your code that will be valid for that given location. It is also referred to as *list members*.

Complete word is very similar to statement completion, but without the UI. If the method or object you are typing is unique, complete word will fill out the word for you, even if statement completion is not showing. Complete word is the equivalent of clicking or hitting Enter on a particular method or object in statement completion.

I always have to go back and look up the difference between parameter info and quick info. Quick info displays a ToolTip with information about the given method or object. It is the ToolTip you see when you hover over a method or object. Parameter info is a little more self-explanatory. It is the ToolTip you see when you are filling in the parameters to your method call.

Tip 2.30: You can use Ctrl+J to invoke statement completion

The keyboard shortcut to invoke statement completion is Ctrl+J, which is bound to the command *Edit.ListMembers*.

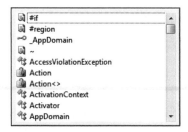

In the Text Editor toolbar, you can invoke statement completion via the Show Member List icon.

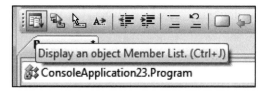

Tip 2.31: How to display parameter info for a function

Press Ctrl+Shift+Space to display the parameter info. The command is *Edit.ParameterInfo*.

```
            static void Main(string[] args)
            {
                Console.WriteLine("Hello World");
            }      ◀1 of 19▶  void Console.WriteLine ()
                   Writes the current line terminator to the standard output stream.
```

To iterate through the possible parameter choices, press the down arrow to go to the next function overload and press the up arrow to go to the previous function overload. For whatever reason, I always reverse these arrow keys and end up navigating backward.

Tip 2.32: How to display quick info for a function

Type in a method name—for example, **Console.Read**—and then press Ctrl+K, Ctrl+I to invoke Quick Info on a function. The command is *Edit.QuickInfo*.

```
        static·void·Main(string[]·args)
        {
            Console.Read();
        }
                        int Console.Read()
        static·strin   Reads the next character from the standard input stream.
        {
                        Exceptions:
            return·"     System.IO.IOException
        }
```

Tip 2.33: How to complete a word

Whenever you can invoke statement completion, you can also execute the *Edit. CompleteWord* command. This command completes a word that is partially complete and that has no other possibilities. And if there are other multiple possibilities, the command invokes statement completion.

In the following example, since Console.WriteL has no possible matches other than Console. WriteLine, pressing Ctrl+Space or Alt+Right Arrow will write out WriteLine.

```
        static·void·Main(string[]·args)
        {
            Console.WriteL
        }
```

Tip 2.34: How to increase the statement completion font size

Go to Tools–Options–Environment–Fonts And Colors and set the Show Settings For option to Statement Completion. Now you can modify the font and font size.

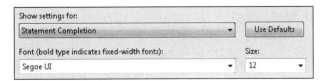

This is the statement completion box at font size 12.

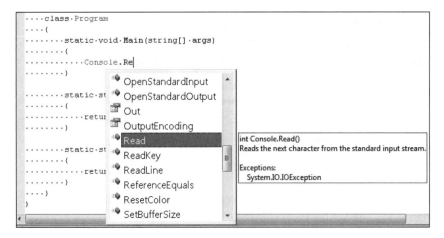

Tip 2.35: You can resize the statement completion dialog box

It's all about the simple things in life.

Yep, you can resize the statement completion dialog box from any direction.

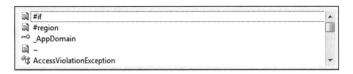

A couple of things to note:

- Max height is limited to one-third of the screen size.

- Although width is resizable, only height is persisted.

Tip 2.36: You can toggle between the Common and All Statement Completion tabs via the keyboard

Once the statement completion dialog box is up, press Alt+. to move to the All tab and Alt+, to move to the Common tab.

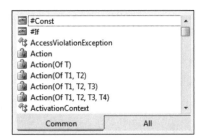

Tip 2.37: How to turn off IntelliSense by default

Just in case you ever need to do this....

Go to Tools–Options–Text Editor–All Languages–General and uncheck Auto List Members and Parameter Information. If you just want to disable IntelliSense by default for a particular language, go to the Text Editor–*<language>*–General option page and set the behavior there.

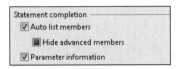

Note that the IntelliSense commands themselves are not disabled, meaning you can still invoke IntelliSense via the keyboard shortcut or a toolbar button.

Code Snippets

The only thing I like more than breaking software is leaving a note that I broke the software. For example, when I first took over testing code snippets, I would attempt to break the UI by doing all kinds of unexpected things, like trying to type "Sara wuz here" in place of a code snippet name. Most of my attempts were unsuccessful, as you would expect, but eventually I did find a series of keyboard shortcuts that led to a crash.

The cool thing about software testing is that once you find one bug, there's usually a collection of bugs nearby. All you have to do is know how to find the bug pattern. Expanding on this series of UI interactions, I ended up finding at least three crashes that day, all with "Sara wuz here" in the reproduction steps and in the screen shots for the developer to enjoy.

Fortunately, it was a Friday afternoon, so I had to avoid the developer for only a few hours. =D

Using Code Snippets

These next tips walk you through inserting and managing code snippets.

Tip 2.38: You can use Ctrl+K, Ctrl+X to insert a code snippet

The keyboard shortcut to insert a code snippet is Ctrl+K, Ctrl+X. It is bound to the command *Edit.InsertSnippet*, in case your mileage varies, depending on your configuration settings.

I'm going to use C# for this tip, but this tip applies to all languages that support code snippets. When I invoke the *Edit.InsertSnippet* command, the code snippet insertion UI pops up. The real tip here is that the snippet picker allows for type-ahead selection. Note how I started typing "#re" on the line. (Oh, the fun I had testing this . . . but I digress.)

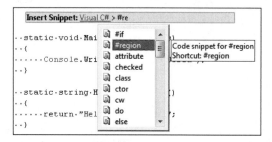

Additional keystrokes:

- You can hit Tab to autocomplete the word. If the word happens to be the code snippet (and not a folder), pressing Tab will insert it.

- You can also hit Shift+Tab to navigate back to the previous word (my contribution to the insertion UI).

Tip 2.39: You can insert a code snippet via its shortcut keyword

Code snippets have the support to be given a "shortcut," usually an abbreviated version of the code snippet name that you can type into the editor and hit Tab to insert.

To insert, simply type in the name of the snippet—for example, **for**—and then hit Tab. Note that if statement completion is open, you'll have to hit Tab twice to insert the snippet.

In both Visual Studio 2005 and 2008, you'll be able to see C# Code Snippet shortcuts in the statement completion window. The following screen shot is the *for* snippet displayed within the statement completion window. Note the snippet icon to the left.

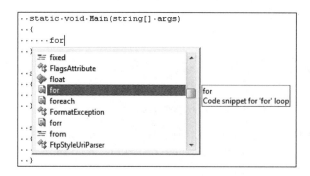

In Visual Studio 2008, you won't see Visual Basic snippets in the statement completion window, but you will see a note in the ToolTip when you can hit Tab twice to insert the corresponding snippet.

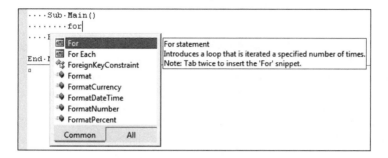

Tip 2.40: You can insert a snippet by pressing Tab Tab

> **Sara Aside** A few months ago, I had dinner with some Microsoft MVPs and other Visual Studio users who were on campus for the Microsoft certification exams. One of the developers said, "Hey Sara, you need to blog about Snippet Tab Tab." I was blown away. I had tested this feature inside and out and never had heard of "Tab Tab." It turns out that he was just referring to the sequence of keystrokes you use to insert a snippet, but I never even thought to refer to it as the "Tab Tab" feature.

I'm not a C# developer. I spent the majority of my time writing code in Visual Basic during my software testing days. Whenever I need to use C#, I heavily rely upon code snippets because I don't recall the syntax off the top of my head.

When in the appropriate place in the editor, you can type in the keyboard shortcut of a snippet, like **for**.

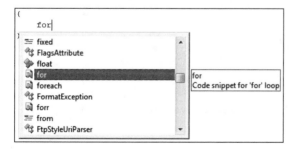

In this state, you can simply press Tab twice to insert the snippet.

Why twice? Press it once to autocomplete statement completion. If you just type **f** for "for", and *for* is highlighted, you can just press Tab once to complete the word *for*. Press it twice to generate the snippet, since the cursor will be at the end of the word *for* in the editor.

```
for (int i = 0; i < length; i++)
{

}
```

And the moral of the story is "*<snippet>* Tab Tab."

Tip 2.41: How to browse code snippets and add new ones

All code snippets are found in the Code Snippets Manager. It is found at Tools–Code Snippets Manager. If you are using the General Development Settings, you can use Ctrl+K, Ctrl+B to bring up the dialog box.

In my opinion, the most useful aspect of this dialog box is to browse through your current snippets to learn what the shortcuts are to quickly insert the snippet into the editor.

Additionally, this is where you add (a directory of snippets) and import (a single snippet or multiple-selected snippets to a specified folder via the Import Code Snippet dialog box).

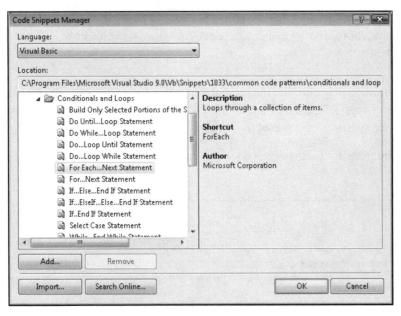

You should always check to see what type of snippets you are browsing by looking at the Language combo box found at the top of the dialog box. The Code Snippets Manager Language combo box is an MRU list, meaning that the last set of snippets you looked at (let's say XML) will come up the next time you bring up the dialog box.

> **Sara Aside** For me as a tester, it was critical that I always confirmed where I was before using the dialog box; otherwise, I would end up logging incorrect bugs. Maybe you don't need this warning, but old habits die hard.

Tip 2.42: How to change default values and variables in a code snippet

When you insert a code snippet, the editor highlights the fields (variables, values, and so on) you can modify depending on how the code snippet was written. The idea is you modify the contents of the field and then press Tab to navigate to the next field. When you press Tab, that particular field is updated throughout the entire snippet. You can also navigate outside the field via the arrow keys to invoke the update.

```
static void Main(string[] args)
{
    for (int i = 0; i < length; i++)
    {

    }
}
```

If you press Enter, however, you will be committing both the current change (if any) and the entire snippet, meaning you can't use undo to get back to those highlighted fields. You would have to use your favorite refactoring method to make any additional updates.

Tip 2.43: How to share code snippets with your team

> **Sara Aside** I like this tip because it isn't really about how to use features but rather how to combine features to do new things.

To share code snippets among others on your team:

1. Go to Tools–Code Snippets Manager, press the Add button, and type in the UNC share name.

2. Go to Tools–Import And Export Settings, Export, and choose to export just the Code Snippets Locations to a file.

3. Send out that .vssettings file to those on your team. They can go to Tools–Import And Export Settings and choose Import to retrieve it.

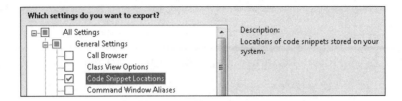

Tip 2.44: How to insert a code snippet around a block of code

C# and XML support the *Edit.SurroundWith* command that will insert the desired snippet around the selected code (whether it is just a selected word, selected line, or entire function). The keyboard shortcut is Ctrl+K, Ctrl+S.

For example, the following illustration shows how to use the Surround With feature to insert a *for* loop around an existing *for* loop.

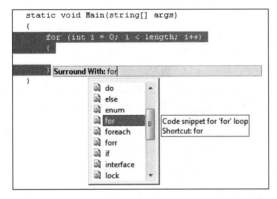

The result is a *for* loop inside a *for* loop, as shown here:

```
static void Main(string[] args)
{
    for (int i = 0; i < length; i++)
    {
        for (int i = 0; i < length; i++)
        {

        }
    }
}
```

Chapter 3
Find What You Are Searching For

I didn't spend too much time testing the Find features in the editor, as I was more focused on core editing and Microsoft IntelliSense functionality. However, there were times when I helped to analyze test-case failures, assisted in the full test pass, or just did what we call a *bug bash*, where the test team devotes an entire working day (if not the entire 24 hours) to try to find as many bugs as possible.

You can categorize searching within the editor into three buckets: keyboard searches, quick searches, and advanced searches. The keyboard searches tend to be the fastest, involving the least amount of interaction with the user interface (UI), but they can be limited in scope. The quick searches are your multipurpose searches. But, depending on what you are searching for and where you want to look for it, there may be a more efficient job search. And finally, the advanced searches—namely, Find In Files—are your Swiss army knife of search function-ality, especially when you need to search anywhere for anything on the hard drive.

Searches from the Keyboard

The tips covered in this section are designed to limit the amount of UI you need to interact with to conduct a search. Avoiding UI interactions tends to save time, especially when you are repeating the action frequently throughout the day.

Incremental Search

Incremental search is a powerful search to use when you want to keep both your focus and your cursor in the editor when searching in the current document. It is powerful because it allows you to keep typing, meaning the search is driven by keystrokes. And you don't need to interact with any UI.

Tip 3.1: How to behold the power of incremental search

> **Sara Aside** I didn't know about incremental search until someone showed me. Now I can't live without it.

To conduct an incremental search, follow these steps:

1. Press Ctrl+I.

2. Start typing the text you are searching for.

Note You'll see the cursor jump to the first match, highlighting the current search string.

3. Press Ctrl+I again to jump to the next occurrence of the search string.

Additionally, you can press Ctrl+Shift+I to search backward.

To stop searching, press Esc. You'll see confirmation in the status bar that you are out of the incremental search mode.

Current Word Searches

These next tips illustrate what you can do and what you can customize when searching a currently-selected word.

Tip 3.2: You can use Ctrl+F3 to search for the currently-selected word without bringing up the Find And Replace window

Just select some text (or just have the cursor on the word you want to search for) and press Ctrl+F3. Ctrl+Shift+F3 will do a reverse search.

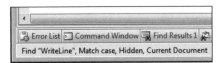

Note that a Ctrl+F3 search uses the following options:

- Is case sensitive
- Searches hidden text
- Allows for partial matching
- Does not use regular expressions

Tip 3.3: How to not automatically search for the currently-selected word

Go to the Tools–Options–Environment–Find And Replace page, and uncheck the Automatically Populate Find What With Text From The Editor option.

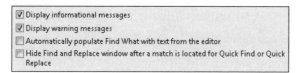

Now, when you hit Ctrl+F (Quick Find) or Ctrl+Shift+F (Find In Files) or Ctrl+H (Quick Replace), the Find What combo box will not automatically display the current word or selected text.

Repeat Last Search

Reducing the number of necessary keystrokes in a commonly repeated action saves time in the long run. Repeating the last search is definitely one of the ways you can take advantage of this philosophy. Instead of having to redo the last search, which may take several keystrokes and even involve using the UI, you can press a single keyboard shortcut to search what you last searched for.

Tip 3.4: You can use F3 to search for the last thing you searched for

Obviously, you can press the Find Next button in the Find And Replace window. But you can also press F3 to search for the next instance, and Shift+F3 searches for the previous instance of the search string.

Note that this keyboard shortcut is only for Quick Find and Find In Files, not for an incremental search.

Quick Searches

Quick Find and Quick Replace can be considered as all-purpose, generic searches. Where incremental search is the most focused search and Find In Files is the most comprehensive search, the following "Quick" search-and-replace features are in the middle of the road.

Quick Find

Quick Find is your standard Ctrl+F search, as represented in most of today's software applications.

Tip 3.5: You can use Ctrl+F to use Quick Find in the current document

Pressing Ctrl+F brings up the UI to start a Quick Find search in the current document.

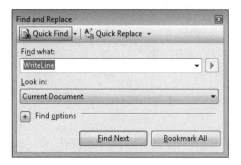

Quick Find prepopulates the Find What text with whatever text is selected in the editor or the word that the cursor is currently on.

Additionally, this Find And Replace window is actually a tool window, so you can dock it somewhere and continue to type in the editor while the window is open.

Tip 3.6: How to use the Find combo box to do a Quick Find in the current document

The Find combo box is another way of doing a Quick Find with the scope limited to the current document.

Press Ctrl+D to reach the Find Combo box. Now type whatever search string you want, and press Enter to do a forward search or Shift+Enter to do a reverse search.

Tip 3.7: How to customize the Find combo box (Ctrl+D) search

Press Ctrl+F to bring up the Quick Find window and expand the Find Options section. These options also control the Find combo box.

Quick Replace

The Quick Replace feature uses a Quick Find to find all the occurrences of the search term and then replace them with the desired text.

Tip 3.8: You can use Ctrl+H to bring up the Quick Replace window

Press Ctrl+H to bring up the Quick Replace window. The command is *Edit.Replace*. You need to press either the Replace button or the Replace All button to start the find-and-replace action.

Additionally, you can customize your find-and-replace experience by expanding the Find Options section.

Tip 3.9: How to hide the Quick Find/Quick Replace window after the first search hit

Let's say you are searching for some text, and you want the Ctrl+F Quick Find window or the Ctrl+H Quick Replace window to disappear after the first search.

Go to the Tools–Options–Environment–Find And Replace page, and check the Hide Find And Replace Window After A Match Is Located For Quick Find Or Quick Replace option.

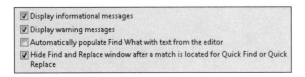

Quick Symbol

And the final search feature that's labeled as "quick" is for searching for symbols, whether it is in your solution or in the entire Microsoft .NET Framework.

Tip 3.10: How to search for a symbol

The final search command is *Edit.FindSymbol*, bound to Alt+F12. Using this command, you can search within your current solution (including or excluding references), or even within the .NET Framework.

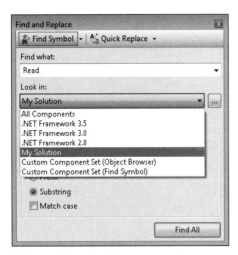

Tip 3.11: You can use Shift+Alt+F12 to use Find Symbol

Like in the previous tip about Find Symbol, select a word in the editor you want to use Find Symbol with and then press Shift+Alt+F12. No Find Symbol window will appear. It is bound to *Edit.QuickFindSymbol*.

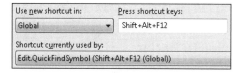

Shift+Alt+F12 uses the same customizations in the Find Symbol window. So, if you need to change the scope for Find Symbol, make the customization in the Find Symbol window.

Find In Files Searches

Find In Files and Find And Replace represent the most advanced search-and-replace functionality in the editor. This section covers the ins and outs of using these searches, while providing tips for associated features, such as the Find Results window.

Find In Files

Find In Files has the most options and will search the broadest scope, including files located on your computer that live outside the solution.

Tip 3.12: How to find in files

Press Ctrl+Shift+F to bring up the Find In Files window.

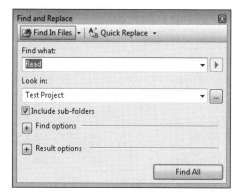

Additionally, you can type in text in the Find combo box and click the Find In Files icon to the left of it, as shown here:

There are a lot of options associated with Find In Files, which I'll cover in this chapter.

Tip 3.13: You can customize what files to find in

With the Find In Files window showing, change the Look In combo box to anything except Current Document or All Open Documents. This enables the Look At These File Types option, allowing you to select what file types to search for.

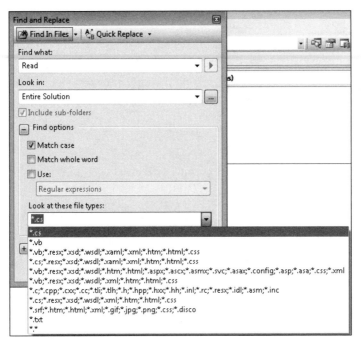

And for a more advanced searching experience, there's a "..." button next to the Look In combo box.

Clicking this button pops up the Choose Search Folders window. Here you can create a set of folders to search in.

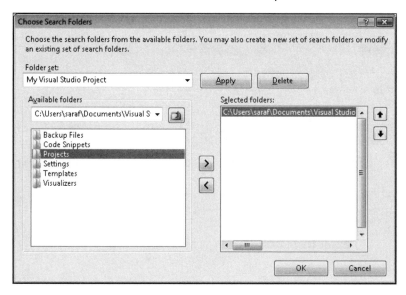

And now you can find your custom folder set as a Look In option.

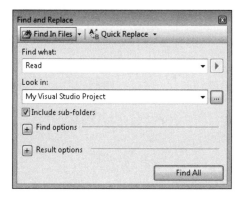

Tip 3.14: You can stop a Find In Files search

Press the keyboard chord Alt+F3, S to stop a background search. The command is *Edit. StopSearch*.

You can also press the Stops A Background Find toolbar icon on the Find Results window.

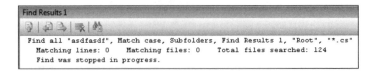

Tip 3.15: You can replace all search string occurrences in files

Just like Ctrl+H performs a Quick Replace, Ctrl+Shift+H brings up the Replace In Files window.

Note that another option, Keep Modified Files Open After Replace All, appears in the Result Options section.

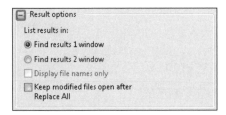

Obviously, if you check this option, all modified files will be opened in the editor. The significance of this is that you can use the undo command if you change your mind.

Find And Replace

The Find And Replace feature uses Find In Files to find all the occurrences of the search term and then replace it with the desired text.

Tip 3.16: How to dock the Find And Replace window

The Find And Replace window is not a dialog box, but actually a tool window. Thus, you can dock it to the side if you find it in your way. Since this window begins in a floating state, it may not be obvious that you can dock it.

Right-click the tool window title bar and select Dockable. Now the tool window can be docked using a docking target. Additionally, you can go to the Window menu and select Dockable.

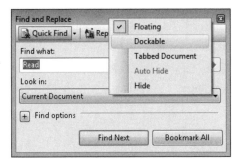

Find Results Window

Using the Find In Files search returns all search hits in the Find Results tool window.

Tip 3.17: You can use F8 to navigate the Find Results window

You can use F8 (with the focus either in the Find Results window or in the editor) to navigate to the next result, or you can use Shift+F8 to go to the previous result. The commands are *Edit.GoToNextLocation* and *Edit.GoToPrevLocation*.

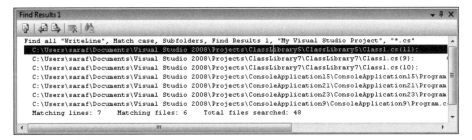

And yes, you can use Quick Find, using Ctrl+F, within the Find Results window.

Tip 3.18: How to show and hide find messages

Far too often, I uncheck the Always Show This Message check box, not knowing how to get the message back.

For Find And Replace, you can specify whether to hide or show these message boxes on the Tools–Options–Environment–Find And Replace page. The options are Display Informational Messages and Display Warning Messages.

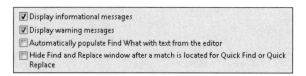

Informational messages are those "FYI—for your information" style messages. Examples include "No more occurrences found," "The specified text was not found," "Find reached the starting point," and so forth. They are indicated by a blue "i" in a white circle.

Warning messages are those that ask a question along the lines of "Are you sure?" For example, "Do you want to cancel?", "Do you want to open files when you perform a find and replace in closed files to enable undo?", and so forth. They are indicated by a yellow triangle with an exclamation point in the middle.

Tip 3.19: How to browse Find Symbol results

The results of a Find Symbol or a Quick Find Symbol action appear in the Find Symbol Results window. Press Ctrl+Alt+F12 to bring up the Find Symbol Results window. The command is *View.FindSymbolResults*.

- Press F8 to navigate to the next result, and press Shift+F8 to navigate to the previous result. The commands are *Edit.GoToNextLocation* and *Edit.GoToPreviousLocation*, respectively.

- Press F12 within the Find Symbol Results window to jump to the definition for the symbol in the editor. The command is *Edit.GoToDefinition*.

Additionally, you can right-click the symbol to bring up the context menu and select Browse Definition to view the symbol in the Object Browser. This command is *Edit.BrowseDefinition*, in case you want to bind it to a keyboard shortcut.

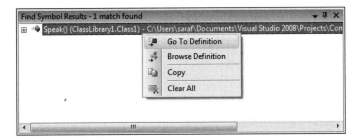

Other Search Options

This section provides tips for searching hidden text, expanding or limiting your search scope, and using regular expressions.

Hidden Text

The Find And Replace window provides a way to enable or disable searching within hidden text.

Tip 3.20: How to search hidden text in the editor

Press Ctrl+F to bring up the Find And Replace window. You can then expand the Find Options section and select Search Hidden Text.

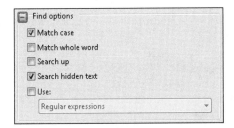

This is usually the first option I set (or I verify it is set).

Search Scope

You can select the scope of your search, including the current code block, the current document, all open documents, the current project, and the entire solution.

Tip 3.21: How to search within the current project or entire solution

Press Ctrl+F to open the Quick Find window. Then click the arrow to display the drop-down list for the Look In combo box to select the search scope.

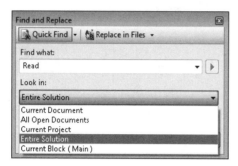

Regular Expressions

You can search using either wildcards or regular expressions in the Find And Replace window.

Tip 3.22: How to use wildcards and regular expressions while searching

In the Find And Replace window, expand the Find Options node and check the Use check box. This option enables you to select either wildcards or regular expressions.

Now that little grayed-out arrow, which is called an expression builder and is located next to the Find What text box, is enabled. In case you're like me and don't use regular expressions all that often, the expression builder can be a great little cheat sheet.

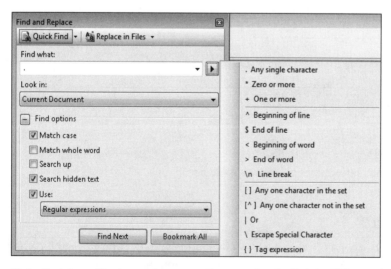

Note that the editor's regular expressions engine is slightly different from the .NET Framework regular expressions engine; hence, the cheat sheet may really come in handy.

Chapter 4
Manage Your Environment Layout

The window management feature area for Microsoft Visual Studio represents the basic functionality for tool windows, document windows, and menu and command bars. As the feature area tester on the Visual Studio Core team, I covered the breadth of the window management features, which included generic scenarios such as tool window docking and autohiding. It was the responsibility of the language teams to focus on depth testing for their particular scenarios.

Window management was one of my favorite feature areas to test. Because the feature area was so large and there were so many UI combinations to choose from, I got to be creative in the ways I found bugs. I loved coming up with new ways to break stuff and then getting to log the bugs. Testing is the ultimate "Hey developer, you broke it and I'm telling" experience. And not surprisingly, my favorite bug of all time comes from this area.

We had one particular tool window test case that test performance under stress by attempting to dock a tool window to the same dock target many, many times in a row. What was cool was how the tool window client area, the UI within the tool window, would get smaller and smaller with each dock after approximately 100 times. Then, at some point, the client area would somehow draw itself with a negative size and paint over the tool window title bar—quite odd. Obviously, the test began to fail at this point because the automation framework couldn't find the tool window title bar. I'll never forget looking at the screen shot captured at that point of the test case failure and seeing this half-eaten title bar. It was such a cool bug. Of course, it took what felt like forever to get "the repro," which is the term we use to describe the exact steps needed to reproduce the bug. Having to dock a tool window 100 times gets very old very quickly when doing it by hand, but it was well worth doing it when I finally did get that repro.

Document Windows

A document window is any window that is opened in the center of the IDE. It has a file tab and behaves just as any opened file would. Obvious examples include files and designers. Not-so-obvious examples include the project properties and tool windows in a tabbed document state. And note that any tool window can act as a document window, but not vice versa.

File Tab Channel

The file tab channel is the UI strip that contains all the file tabs for the open documents. It also contains a lot of quick shortcuts and powerful commands for manipulating and navigating files.

Tip 4.1: You can use Ctrl+Alt+Down Arrow to drop down the file tab channel file menu

A fellow program manager and I were trying to out "Did you know..." each other about Visual Studio the other day in my office. I won with this one:

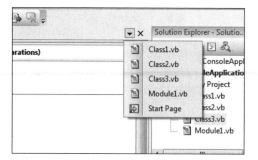

On the file tab channel, all the way to the right side, there's an inverted triangle (that is, a drop-down arrow) that, when pressed, invokes the File menu drop-down list.

There are two "Did you know..." points here:

- **You can press Ctrl+Alt+Down Arrow to show the File menu drop-down list**   This keyboard shortcut is bound to the global scope, meaning you can press this chord anywhere in the IDE and get the File menu drop-down list to appear. The command is *Window.ShowEzMDIFileList*. In case you are curious, *EzMDI* stands for Easy MDI, representing the default tabbed document view rather than the multiple documents view, or MDI (multiple document interface).

- **The File menu drop-down list supports type-ahead selection**   If you have a lot of files listed, you can type the name of the file, and when there's an exact match (meaning there isn't a conflict), the focus will jump to that file in the list, allowing you to hit Enter to open it.

Tip 4.2: You can use Close All But This on files in the file tab channel

This is a really, really useful feature, but I'll always remember how difficult it was for me to find bugs with it. That really frustrates a tester, when you can't break a developer's newly written code.

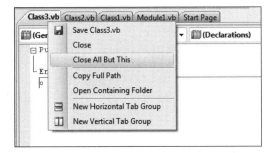

Right-click a file tab, and select Close All But This. This command closes all the other files in the editor, except for the currently active file, obviously.

And yes, you can bind it to a keyboard shortcut. The command is *File.CloseAllButThis*. In the General Development Settings, this isn't bound to any keyboard shortcut, so have fun!

Tip 4.3: You can copy a file's full path from the file tab channel

Now this is a feature I absolutely cannot live without. This was one of the best features added in Visual Studio 2005 (in my humble, biased opinion).

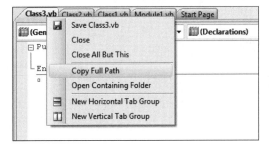

On the file tab channel, you can right-click and select Copy Full Path—voilà, you have the full path for that file.

In previous versions of Visual Studio (such as Visual Studio .NET 2003), you had to go to the Properties window and copy the full path from there. In even earlier versions, well, um, I don't recall. (I started working at Microsoft in September 2001.)

Tip 4.4: You can open a Windows Explorer browser directly to the active file

Right-click any file tab, and select Open Containing Folder. I love this feature, although it is my second favorite tip. The previous Tip 4.3 is my all-time favorite. It's great to be able to jump from the file to the folder on disk to look for stuff, to change attributes on the file, to do a rename, or whatever else. It is very, very useful.

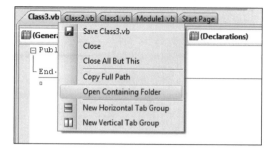

Tip 4.5: How to close just the selected files you want

Okay, this is not one of my better "Tip of the Day" titles, but it's my way of introducing the Window Windows dialog box. It is such a simple dialog box, but for some reason I loved testing it. Maybe it was because it didn't have that many (if any) automated test-case failures to analyze.

You can bring up the Window Windows dialog box by choosing Windows from the Window menu.

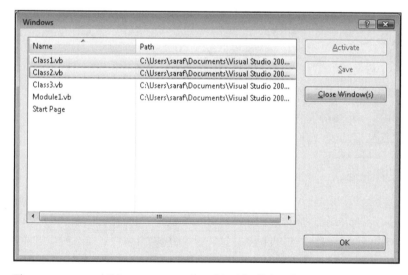

There are several things you can do with this dialog box:

- Select which files you want to close, in case the Close All But This command doesn't meet your needs. That's my best tip on why and when to use this dialog box.

- Select which file to activate; but there are numerous faster ways to do this.

- Select which files you want to save; but then again, you would most likely use Save All.

When you're working in MDI mode, you get an additional two buttons: Tile Horizontally and Tile Vertically.

See Tip 4.12 for more information.

I strongly recommend using Window Windows for navigation if you are using any sort of accessibility options or assistive technologies (for example, screen readers, screen magnifiers). Window Windows provides an easy and quick way to navigate among files and to close files.

Tip 4.6: Under what condition does the file tab channel drop-down button change its icon?

Next you see a picture containing the right portion of the file tab channel. The drop-down arrow to the right of the tabs drops down the list of open files.

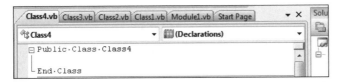

Now, when does a bar appear over the drop-down arrow (as shown next)?

When at least one file tab has fallen off the file tab channel, the icon will change, representing the hidden file or files.

IDE Navigator

In Visual Studio 2005, we introduced the IDE Navigator. It's that window that pops up when you press Ctrl+Tab. When the window pops up, keep holding down the Ctrl key while you use either the arrow keys or the mouse to pick a file or tool window to activate.

Tip 4.7: You can use Ctrl+Tab to bring up the IDE Navigator to get a bird's-eye view of and navigate all open files and tool windows

The IDE Navigator is bound to the *Window.NextDocumentWindowNav* command, in case you want to change it. I know some settings have Ctrl+Tab bound to *Window.NextDocumentWindow* (no *Nav*).

In Visual Studio 2008, they (since I technically didn't work on that version of Visual Studio) did a lot of UI tweaks with the IDE Navigator. You'll notice that there's more *real estate* (which is what we call the actual space in a UI dialog box), so you can see more of the file path. And of course, there's the preview window, which is pretty cool. (I said "Oooh!" when I first saw it, but I'm a little biased.)

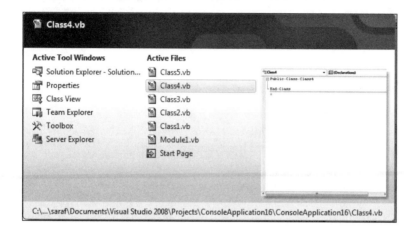

Tip 4.8: How to disable the IDE Navigator

The IDE Navigator isn't for everyone. Some developers prefer that Ctrl+Tab quickly cycle through all their open documents instead of flashing an additional piece of UI.

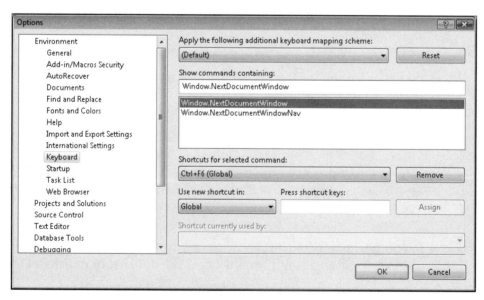

To disable the IDE Navigator, do this:

1. Open Tools–Options–Environment–Keyboard.

2. Under Show Commands Containing, type **Window.NextDocumentWindowNav**.

3. Click the Remove button to remove the Ctrl+Tab keyboard shortcut binding.

To go back to previous Visual Studio Ctrl+Tab behavior, do the following:

1. Under Show Commands Containing, type **Window.NextDocumentWindow**.

2. Position the cursor in the Press Shortcut Keys box, and then press **Ctrl+Tab**.

3. Click Assign to bind the keyboard shortcut.

4. Click OK to accept the changes and dismiss the Tools–Options dialog box.

And Ctrl+Tab will cycle through all open documents without the IDE Navigator popping up.

You'll want to remove the Ctrl+Shift+Tab keyboard shortcut from the *Window.PreviousDocumentWindowNav* command and bind it to the *Window.PreviousDocumentWindow* command instead so that you can have both forward and backward navigation in the file tab channel.

Keyboard Navigation

There are keyboard shortcuts for navigating among the various documents opened in your editor. All the keyboard shortcuts are customizable on the Tools–Options–Environment–Keyboard page.

Tip 4.9: You can use Ctrl+F6 and Ctrl+Shift+F6 to navigate among opened document windows

> **Sara Aside** This tip was posted on Mardi Gras Day 2008, while I was back home celebrating carnival. Happy Mardi Gras, y'all, from New Orleans!!

Similar to Ctrl+Tab functionality, Ctrl+F6 and Ctrl+Shift+F6 allow you to navigate to the next and previous opened documents, respectively, based on a most-recently used sort order. One clear difference here is that the IDE Navigator does not appear, unlike when you use Ctrl+Tab.

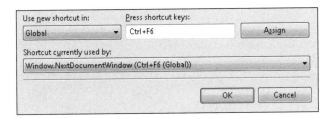

Tip 4.10: You can use Ctrl+F4 to close the current document opened in the editor

If you are using the General Development Settings, the command *Window.CloseDocumentWindow* is bound to Ctrl+F4. This will close the current document.

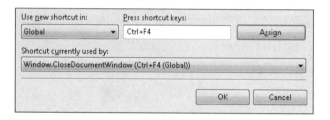

MDI Mode

As already mentioned, *MDI* stands for *Multiple Document Interface*. Early versions of Windows were MDI-mode based, with the classic minimize, maximize, and close buttons in the upper-right corner. In an MDI interface, you can have multiple files opened, where you can tile horizontally and tile vertically. Visual Studio, by default, uses what we call tabbed documents. The code name is *ezMDI*, but this is one of the few places where you'll see the command referred to as such.

Tip 4.11: How to enter MDI mode

There's a setting to toggle Visual Studio from the default tabbed documents mode to the MDI mode. Go to the Tools–Options–Environment–General page, and select Multiple Documents under Window Layout.

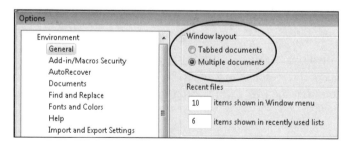

For you Visual Studio .NET 2003 users, you may remember that you had to restart Visual Studio to use MDI. We fixed this (well, the developer fixed it and I tested it) in Visual Studio 2005, so restarting Visual Studio is no longer required.

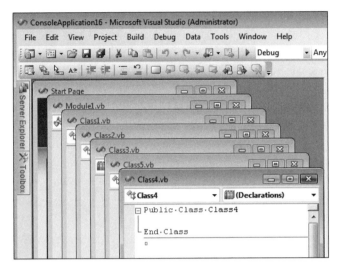

If you're familiar with MDI mode, you might ask, "Can you tile horizontally or vertically? Can you cascade?" Go to the Window menu, and you'll find new options.

Note that both Auto Hide All and Reset Window Layout apply to tool windows. The Cascade, Tile Horizontally, Tile Vertically, and Close All Documents commands apply to document editors, designers, and any tool windows in a tabbed document state.

Tip 4.12: How to show the Tile Horizontally and Tile Vertically buttons in the Window Windows dialog box

> **Sara Aside**   When I initially wrote this tip, I had a nightmare that I broke my consecutive tip series on my blog by forgetting to post a tip. Anyway, while writing tips on the window management series, these buttons caught my eye. I recalled how back in the Visual Studio 2005 development stage I had no clue how to activate them. In fact, I nearly opened a bug claiming that they never become available.

Starting in Visual Studio 2005, the IDE hides the Tile Horizontally and Tile Vertically buttons on the Window Windows dialog box until you are in MDI mode (discussed in Tip 4.11) with several files open.

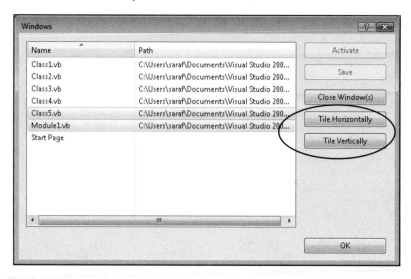

Tool Windows

You know a tool window when you see one. It's basically a helper window that you want to keep around while you perform a task in the IDE. You could think of a tool window as a glorified modeless dialog box (meaning you can click other UI elements outside of the window) with additional functionality that makes it a tool window, such as the ability to dock and autohide.

At a high level, a tool window can be in one of five states: dockable, autohiding, tabbed document, floating, or hidden. These states can be combined and put into special cases to cause the tool window to be in interesting hybrid states, as illustrated in Tip 4.16. But for now, we'll explore the most common of these states.

Dockable State

Prior to Visual Studio 2005, it took some trial and error to dock a tool window where you wanted it. The Visual Studio team would watch usability studies of users trying to complete a task, where the user would be just mere pixels away from docking his tool window successfully but never quite make it. Many of us would nearly fall out of our chairs trying to mentally push the user's mouse pointer to the correct location.

Fortunately, Visual Studio 2005 introduced docking targets, which not only provide a bird's-eye view of what dock positions are available, but also provides a preview of where the tool window will be docked. No more falling out of our chairs.

Tip 4.13: You can choose from nine IDE tool window docking targets

When a tool window is in a dockable state, a set of docking targets appears when you move a tool window to a specific location, such as hovering it over another tool window.

But did you know that there are nine IDE docking targets? These docking targets allow you to pin tool windows to the inner and outer parts of the IDE itself.

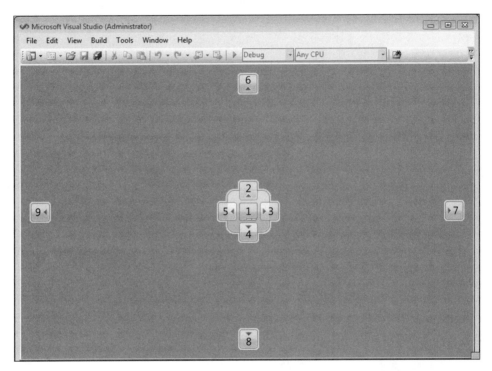

Docking target 1 puts a tool window into a tabbed document state, docking target 3 docks a tool window to the inner right edge, and docking target 7 docks a tool window to the outer right edge.

If there's no tool window docked on the right, targets 7 and 3 seem to be the same. But if you dock tool window A using target 7 and then dock tool window B using target 3, you get tool window A on the outside and tool window B docked to the left side of tool window A.

You have no idea how crazy it was to test all of these combinations! But I loved it nonetheless.

Tip 4.14: How to undock only a single tool window from a group

You can always undock a single tool window by dragging its tool window tab.

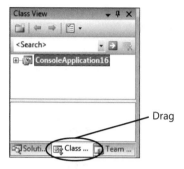

Drag

Tip 4.15: You can dock a tool window to the top of the IDE

I implied this possibility existed in a previous tip when I introduced all the various IDE docking targets (see Tip 4.13). But I wanted to call it out specifically since it is rare to see a tool window in this position.

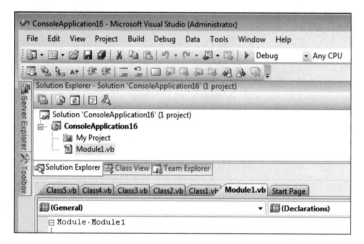

The Memory tool windows (when you're in debugging mode) are the only ones that come to mind right now. But there's nothing preventing you from docking your own tool windows up there, as illustrated with the Solution Explorer in the preceding screen shot.

Tip 4.16: You can use docking targets to dock tool windows in new and crazy ways

Sara Aside Docking targets are hands-down my all-time favorite feature that I tested. Oh, the fun I would have opening bugs like "Tool Window client area resizes to a negative size after redocking to same location 100-plus times." (Yes, the bug was fixed.)

When you drag a tool window over a docking target, you'll get a preview, as you see in the next screen shot.

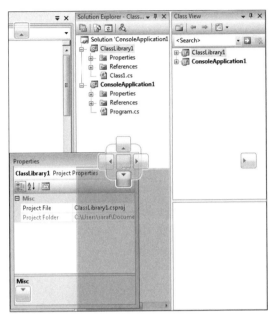

But, let's have a little fun …

I have no idea how the tool window tab group shown next could be useful, but maybe if it were resized to fit a secondary monitor …

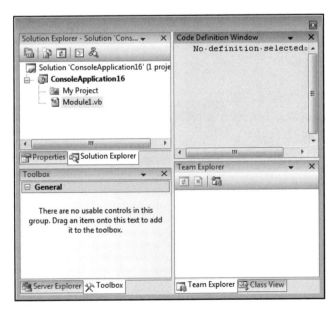

Can you tell I enjoyed being a tester?

Autohiding State

Sometimes you don't want to completely close a tool window, but you don't want it in your way. Autohiding is a nice way of tucking the tool window away but keeping it ready to spring back out whenever the IDE thinks you need it, or whenever you want it to slide back out.

Tip 4.17: You can autohide all of your tool windows with one command

On the Window menu, there's the Auto Hide All command. Your environment can go from looking like the following screen shot, with lots and lots of tool windows open:

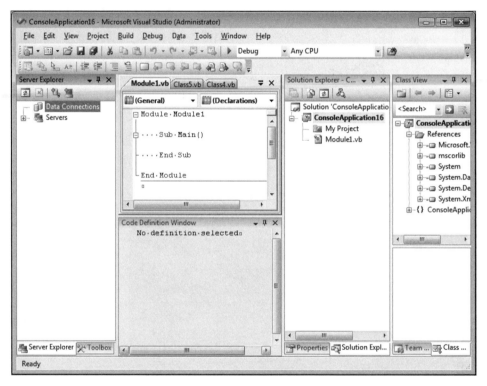

to looking like this screen shot:

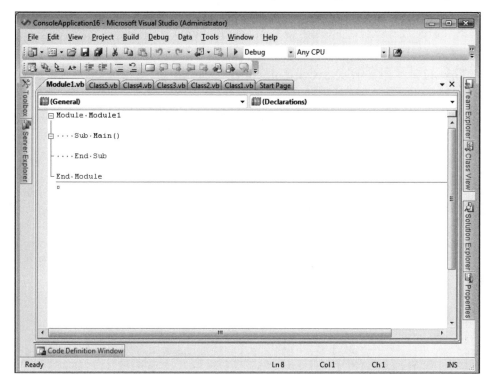

However, there is one caveat: there isn't a command to slide out all of your tool windows.

Tip 4.18: You can customize how pressing a tool window push pin autohides the tool window or tool window tab group

On the Tools–Options–Environment–General page, you'll find the Auto Hide Button Affects Active Tool Window Only option. The next illustration is a snapshot of two tool windows docked together with the Auto Hide push pin circled.

If you want autohide to apply only to Solution Explorer when you click the push pin, enable the option. Otherwise, autohide will apply to both tool windows.

Tip 4.19: You can show autohiding tool windows via the tool window autohide channel

This is one of those features I always forget. The window management developer and I were discussing another tip, when he showed me the autohide channel context menu.

Right-click the tool window autohide channel to invoke the context menu, and click one of the tool windows to slide it out from hiding.

Note in the picture that the Solution Explorer and Class View tabs are side by side, whereas the Properties tab has some space separating it from the other tabs. This is because Solution Explorer and Class View are docked together and the Properties browser is docked next to it, along the edge.

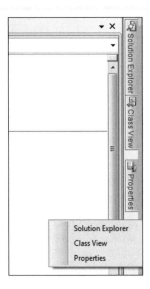

Tip 4.20: You can double-click the tool window title bar to redock the tool window

After you drag a tool window to an undocked position, you can quickly redock the tool window to the previous location by double-clicking the title bar.

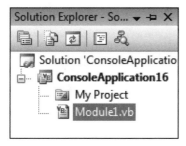

Also, you may notice some tool windows are in tool window groups (as shown in the following image), whereas others are docked individually. To separate a tool window from its group, either drag away or double-click the tool window tab, as shown in the following screen shot.

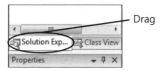

Drag

Tip 4.21: You can use Shift+Click to automatically dock an autohiding tool window

> **Sara Aside**   I thought I had discovered a bug where "Shift+clicking a tool window that is docked at the bottom of the IDE causes the window to disappear instead of docking." But after repro-ing on someone else's machine (it is so important to get a repro on another machine when you are not sure), I realized that it occurred anywhere. Then I realized what the "bug" was…. If the tool window is still sliding out, it will dock. But if the tool window hasn't started to slide out yet, Shift+Click will perform a Hide command. So this tip is based on both behaviors.

Let's start with "Tool Window 101" training. When a tool window is docked (as discussed in Tip 4.13), you have the option to autohide. Just click the autohide push pin as shown in the following image. Or go to the Window menu and choose Auto Hide to autohide the currently selected tool window.

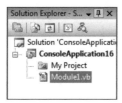

Clicking this push pin causes the window to autohide, as shown here:

You can mouse over the Solution Explorer and click the push pin again to redock. Or you can go to the Window menu and choose Auto Hide, which unchecks the Auto Hide setting. But what's the fun in that?

Now for the actual tip. Did you know that you can press Shift+Click on the autohiding tool window (the second picture in this tip) to move it into a docked state?

However, if the tool window is already sliding out (as shown in the next screen shot), it is automatically hidden.

So you are probably wondering, "Okay Sara, so what is Shift+Click really supposed to do?" It is supposed to perform a *Window.Hide* command. But when the tool window starts to slide, stuff happens in the IDE and it goes into a docked state instead of a hide state.

More than you ever wanted to know about the Visual Studio environment, huh?

Tip 4.22: You can speed up or slow down how fast a tool window slides out from a docked position

On the Tools–Options–Environment–General page, you'll find the Animate Environment Tools check box. This option controls the speed at which a tool window slides in and out of an autohide state.

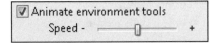

Additionally, you can opt out completely from the animation effect by unchecking the Animate Environment Tools check box. If you do that, tool windows pop to their new locations rather than sliding to them.

Floating State

Floating is very similar to the dockable state, with the exception that docking targets never appear for a tool window that is in a floating state. In the General Development Settings, the Find And Replace window is in a floating state. I've seen questions about how to dock the tool window. To do so, the Find And Replace window must first be put in a dockable state.

Tip 4.23: Why would you want to make a tool window float?

Recall from earlier in this chapter how tool windows are available in five different states:

- Floating
- Dockable
- Tabbed document
- Auto Hide
- Hide

I would say that the dockable state actually represents two mutually exclusive positions the tool window can be in:

- **Docked**   The tool window is locked to a specific location, usually to the side of the IDE.
- **Hovering**   This is my made-up term to describe a tool window that is in the dockable state but is not docked. Recall that the dockable state is different from a floating state, because the floating state cannot be docked.

Most of these states are self-explanatory, especially after a little bit of trial and error, but the floating state may be less obvious. In a floating state, the tool window hovers over the IDE but cannot be docked to a fixed position in the IDE.

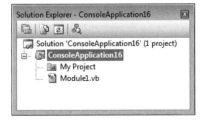

How is this useful? Sometimes you just want to position a tool window in a certain area and, unfortunately, the dock targets appear. If you set it to Floating, you never get docking targets for the tool window. (See Tip 4.13.)

Tabbed Document State

A tool window in a tabbed document state will appear in the file tab channel. I found this behavior most useful with the Output window, as it maximizes the tool window, allowing for the largest amount of text to appear on the screen at one time.

Tip 4.24: How to use Tabbed Document to maximize a tool window

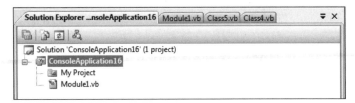

Yet another one of those "Wow, I didn't know you could do that until someone showed me" moments happened when I found out you can maximize a tool window by setting it to a tabbed document state. With your desired tool window selected, either right-click the tool window title bar or tab window to bring up the tool window context menu and then select Tabbed Document. Alternatively, you can go to the Window menu and select Tabbed Document.

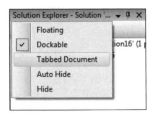

Keyboard Navigation

There are keyboard shortcuts for navigating among the various tool windows opened in your IDE. All the keyboard shortcuts are customizable on the Tools-Options–Environment–Keyboard page.

Tip 4.25: You can use Alt+F7 and Alt+Shift+F7 to move to the next and previous tool windows

The tool windows you open and visit are saved in an MRU (most-recently used) list. So you can navigate among all the various opened tool windows, using Alt+F7 for next and Alt+Shift+F7 for previous.

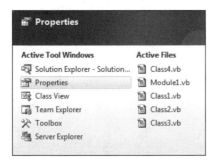

Tip 4.26: You can use Alt+F6 and Alt+Shift+F6 to cycle through opened tool windows

If you don't want the IDE Navigator to appear when you navigate among various opened tool windows, use Alt+F6 and Alt+Shift+F6 to go to the next and previous tool windows, respectively, in most-recently used sort order.

Tip 4.27: How to use Ctrl+Page Up and Ctrl+Page Down to navigate among all the tool windows in a tool window group

Whenever tool window tabs are docked together, they form a little group that you can move around and such, as you've seen in previous tips.

You can use Ctrl+Page Up and Ctrl+Page Down to navigate among the tool windows in this group.

Hide State

A tool window can be in a hidden state, also known as a closed state, by either clicking the X on the tool window title bar, or by selecting Window–Hide.

Tip 4.28: How to customize what clicking the X button does to a tool window or tool window tab group

On the Tools–Options–Environment–General page, you'll find the Close Button Affects Active Tool Window Only check box. The following screen shot shows a snapshot of two tool window tabs docked together, with the close button circled.

If you want only Solution Explorer to close when pressing the X button, enable the option. Otherwise, both tool windows will close.

Hidden Keyboard Shortcuts

I call these "hidden keyboard shortcuts" because the keyboard shortcuts are not bound to a command, meaning you will never find them on the Tools–Options–Environment–Keyboard page. The only way you would find them is if someone told you about them.

I've made an exception for Shift+Esc and included it in this list because I don't think it is very well known, and I'm always shocked whenever I'm reminded about it. I always think it's one of these hidden keyboard shortcuts, but then I realize it's bound to a command.

Tip 4.29: How to drag a tool window around using the keyboard

With the desired tool window selected, press Alt+Minus to bring up the tool window menu. Press the Down Arrow to select the Move command, and press Enter. Now you can control the tool window with the arrow keys.

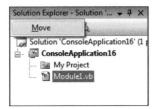

To dock, simply use the arrow keys to get to the desired dock target and hit Enter to commit to docking the tool window to the new location.

Tip 4.30: How to resize a tool window from the keyboard

When a tool window is not docked, follow these steps to resize the window using the keyboard:

1. Press Alt once.

2. Press the Spacebar once. You will get the standard window system menu with Move and Size.

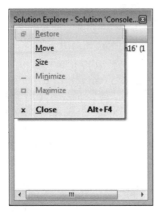

3. Select Size.

4. Press the arrow keys toward the window edge you want to resize, and resize from there.

5. Press Enter to commit to the resizing, or press Esc to cancel the resize changes.

> **Note** Using the Move command from this menu prevents the docking targets from appearing. This is the same as pressing Ctrl and dragging an item using the mouse. If you want to use docking targets via the keyboard, see Tip 4.29.

If you press Alt+Spacebar, you get the main Visual Studio window system menu; this is why you must release the Alt key before you press the Spacebar.

Tip 4.31: How to access a toolbar within a tool window

You may have noticed that within tool windows such as the Solution Explorer, you cannot reach the toolbar by hitting Tab or using the arrow keys. The keyboard shortcut to reach a tool window's toolbar is Shift+Alt. Note that Alt+Shift will *not* work.

Tip 4.32: You can use Shift+Esc to close a tool window

As I've said time and time again on my blog, it's really the simple things in life.... I keep forgetting about this tip, until I see this keyboard shortcut and have to look up what it does.

Use Shift+Esc to close the currently selected tool window. If the focus is not on a tool window but in an editor, and you press Shift+Esc, Visual Studio will just look at you.

Window Layouts

Visual Studio has four window layout states:

- **Design view**   What you see when you launch Visual Studio and start coding.
- **Full screen**   Toggled by Shift+Alt+Enter in the General Development Settings. You can also go to the View menu and click Full Screen. The command is *View.FullScreen*.
- **Debugging view**   Used when debugging.
- **File view**   Used when you open a file via the command line as follows: **devenv.exe myfile.txt**. You'll notice that the environment will have no tool windows showing.

Four Window Layouts

When you shut down Visual Studio in any state, all four states are saved. This includes saving both your tool window layouts and your command bar customizations across all four states. Additionally, all four states are saved when you go to the Tools–Import And Export Settings dialog box and perform an Export of just the Window Layouts category.

Tip 4.33: You can export just your window layouts

You can save all four window layout states at any time by going to the Tools–Import And Export Settings dialog box and choosing the Export option. On the Export page, check the General Settings box and then check the Window Layouts category.

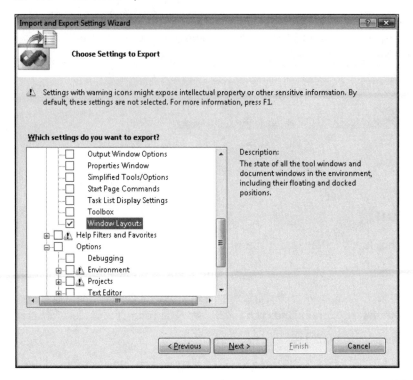

Tip 4.34: How to quickly access Full Screen mode

You can quickly toggle into Full Screen mode from any of the other three window layouts by pressing Shift+Alt+Enter.

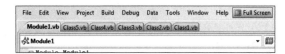

Any window customizations you make in Full Screen mode persist across different window layouts (meaning when you are in design mode and go back to Full Screen mode, you'll see the tool windows where you last had them in Full Screen mode) and across different Visual Studio instances (where you close and reopen the IDE).

Tip 4.35: How to access a file window layout mode that you can customize

You can enter the file window layout mode only by opening a file from a command prompt.

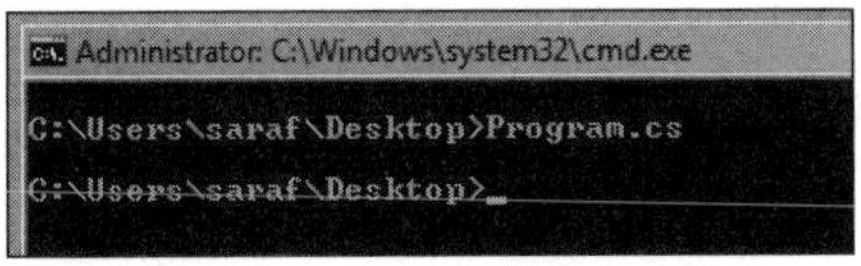

```
Administrator: C:\Windows\system32\cmd.exe

C:\Users\saraf\Desktop>Program.cs

C:\Users\saraf\Desktop>_
```

Invoking **program.cs** from the command prompt opens Visual Studio in this file window layout. You'll note in the following image that there are no tool windows showing and the Text Editor toolbar is showing. This is the default view in the General Development Settings.

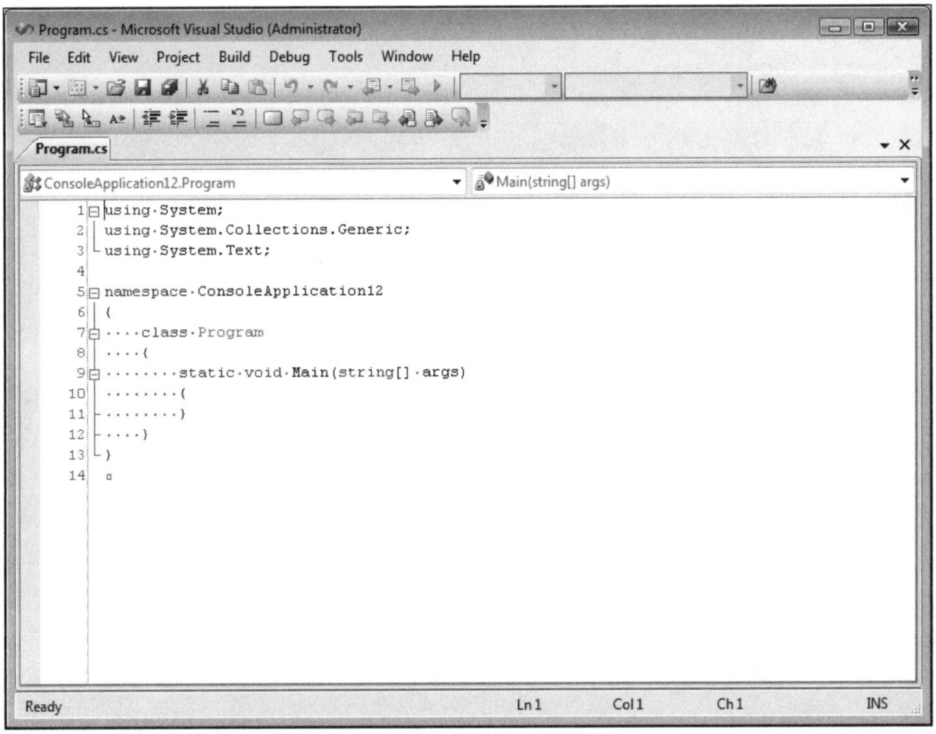

You can make any customizations here and they'll persist across window layout states. (This means that if you open a project, all the tool windows will pop back. This happens because you're now in design mode.) Your customizations will be persisted across sessions. Whenever you shut down Visual Studio, these customizations are saved to disk. They are also saved as a part of your .vssettings file (Tools–Import And Export Settings).

Toolbars and Context Menus

It is common for users to want to tweak every aspect of their IDE, including removing any unwanted commands from their context menus or reducing the number of toolbars that appear at the top of the IDE.

Toolbars

Toolbars are the little strips of buttons, segmented based on the context or task you are performing, such as the buttons for editing code or HTML. They are usually found at the top of the IDE under the File menu, but you can customize these to appear when you want and where you want.

Tip 4.36: You can make a toolbar float

First, you'll want to hover the mouse over the grip control. You'll notice that the mouse control changes to a four-directional pointer.

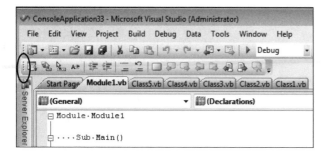

Then hold the primary mouse button down and drag the toolbar out. It'll pop out into a hovering state, as illustrated in the next screen shot. You can also resize its height and width.

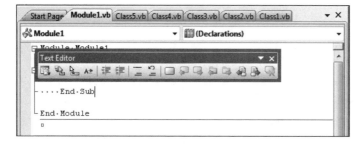

Tip 4.37: You can hide or show the default buttons from any toolbar

Click the drop-down button on the menu, and select Add Or Remove Buttons. You'll be given a choice to either customize the buttons on the given tool window or to bring up the Tools–Customize dialog box. Select the current tool window to see a list of buttons to enable or disable.

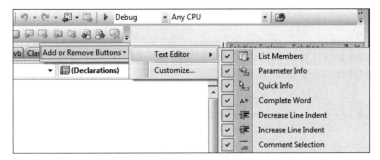

Sometimes, there's no room to see all the available buttons. In that case, you'll see two right-pointing arrows above the drop-down button, as shown in the following image.

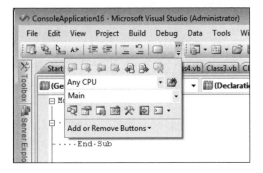

Tip 4.38: How to display any toolbar at any time

Right-click anywhere on the toolbar area, either on a toolbar itself or in the unused portion of the toolbar space, to bring up the context menu of all available toolbars. Then select any toolbar from the list to have it appear.

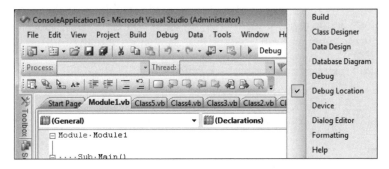

Note that all the buttons may be disabled (as shown in the preceding picture) if you are not in the right environment context, meaning that you don't have the right window, editor, or designer showing to enable the buttons (which is why they were probably hidden to begin with).

But play, experiment, and see if this helps.

Tip 4.39: You can switch and swap buttons on the toolbars while the Tools–Customize dialog box is showing

> **Sara Aside** This is one of my classic moments where I shouted, "Whoa, I never knew this!"

Go to the Tools–Customize dialog box. Note that this is a semi-modal dialog box (my made-up term, although there's probably a real term for it somewhere). A modal dialog box is where you can click only inside the dialog box. But some dialog boxes are modeless, where you can click outside the dialog box and focus remains outside. I call the Tools–Customize dialog box *semi-modal* because you can interact only with the toolbar.

Work with me here. Take your mouse and try to click and drag a button on any toolbar around here, there, and everywhere. Trust me, it will work, even if the Customize dialog box is open. Crazy, huh?

Note that you can even duplicate items by doing a Ctrl+Drag. The duplicate item can even live on a different toolbar!

Tip 4.40: You can show shortcut keys in toolbar ToolTips

Right-click anywhere on any toolbar or toolbar region to bring up the context menu, and then select Customize. In the lower left corner, check Show Shortcut Keys In ScreenTips. Now when you hover over a command, you'll see the keyboard shortcut in the ToolTip.

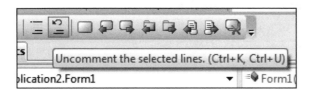

Context Menus

Although it may be obvious that you can customize your toolbars, it may not be as obvious how to customize your context menus.

Tip 4.41: You can customize the commands on the context menus

First, open the Tools–Customize menu. Now select the Toolbars tab, and check Context Menu.

Look up at the toolbar section of Visual Studio. Notice anything different? That's right: you are now looking at your context menus waiting for you to customize them, as shown here:

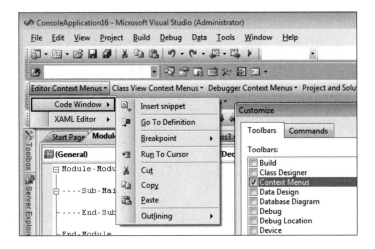

Chapter 5
Discover More Tools for Your Design Time, Part 1

The IDE provides numerous tools beyond those featured in the editor to assist you in designing and writing code. In fact, there are so many tools and tips that I needed two parts to describe them all. Part 1 focuses on tools that are provided as a tool window. Part 2 focuses on tools that are either dialog boxes or Web pages.

Tool Windows

The majority of the tools offered by the IDE exist as tool windows. Unlike a dialog box, where you can interact only with the tool when the dialog box is open, a tool window allows you to quickly toggle between your editor and the tool.

This section covers tips for the Command Window, Toolbox, Task List, Output window, and Object Browser.

Command Window

The Command Window allows you to run Microsoft Visual Studio commands from what looks and feels like an operating system command prompt. For example, instead of going through the Find And Replace window UI to conduct a find, you can use the Command Window to perform the search.

Tip 5.1: You can run Visual Studio commands from the Command Window

Press Ctrl+Alt+A to open the Command Window, or go to View–Other Windows–Command Window. Now you can run various Visual Studio commands without having to go through the menus.

Examples of such commands include the following:

- **>File.Open c:\samples\myFile.txt**   Opens a file without going through the menu
- **>Help vs.commandwindow**   Opens a Help topic directly

- ■ >? i   Returns the contents of the variable *i*

- ■ >? i = 10   Sets the contents of the variable *i*

For more commonly used commands that take arguments for Visual Studio 2008, check out the following documentation: http://msdn2.microsoft.com/en-us/library/c338aexd(VS.90).aspx.

Autocompletion is also provided for both the commands

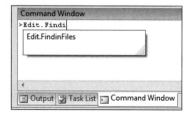

and their corresponding arguments.

Tip 5.2: How to search from the Command Window

Almost all Visual Studio commands can be run via the Command Window, scope willing. The next screen shot shows what the UI looks like when you type in the *Edit.Find* command via the Command Window.

Here are the additional Command Window options:

- **>Edit.Find /options**   Shows which options are currently set

- **>Edit.Find /reset**   Clears all options

Examples of such commands include the following:

- **>Edit.Find MainForm /case /proc**   This is a Quick Find command that matches case in the current procedure.

- **>Edit.Find MainForm /o /w /m /u /h**   This is a Quick Find command that opens documents, matches a whole word, marks matches, searches up, and searches hidden regions, respectively.

- **>Edit.Replace Class1 Class2 /doc /all**   This is a Quick Replace command that replaces all occurrences of Class1 with Class2 in the current document.

- **>Edit.FindInFiles Program /lookin:"c:\Users\saraf\Documents\Visual Studio 2008\ Projects" /ext:*.cs /text2**   This is a Find In Files command that looks in the Projects folder for files with the .cs extension and shows results in the Find Results 2 window.

Tip 5.3: How to log your Command Window session

You can record your Command Window session via the log command. Type **log -on <*filename*>** to start recording. To finish logging, type **log -off**.

There is also an option to overwrite the existing file; if you don't choose this option, the log command appends the text by default.

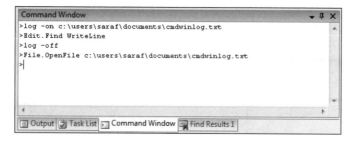

Tip 5.4: How to run external executables from the Command Window

The command *Tools.Shell* runs an external executable out of process from Visual Studio—for example, *Shell <executable>*.

But of course, there are optional arguments. Following are examples of optional arguments for the *Tools.Shell* command:

Shell [/commandwindow] [/dir:folder] [/outputwindow] *<executable>* [/args]

- **/commandwindow** (or **/c**)   Use this command to display the executable's output in the Command Window.

- **/dir:folder**   Use this command to specify the working directory.

- **/outputwindow** (or **/o**)   Use this command to display the executable's output in the Output window.

For example, Shell /o xcopy.exe c:\users\saraf\documents\cmdwinlog.txt c:\users\saraf\logfiles displays the xcopy output in the Output window.

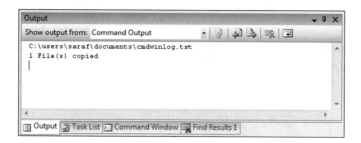

Tip 5.5: How to create a command alias

To create an alias, open the Command Window and type **alias ha Help.About**.

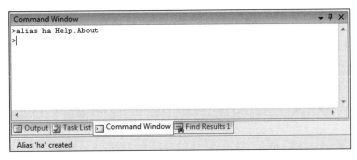

Now typing **ha** in the Command Window pops open the Help–About menu.

But let's explore a more practical application. Consider creating the alias *se* for Solution Explorer, as shown here:

>alias se View.SolutionExplorer

The idea for this example is that while you are coding in the editor, you can press Ctrl+/ to jump to the Find window and type **se**.

Actually, you've probably already used one of the predefined aliases before. The command *Debug.Print* is alias to *?*. To see the full list of aliases, type **alias**.

Finally, to reset your Command Window aliases back to defaults, type **alias /reset**.

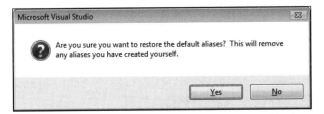

Or you can simply use the */delete* switch to delete a particular alias—for example, type **alias se /delete** to delete that *se* alias.

Output Window

The Output window is commonly used to review the results of your build or to display debugging data. These tips review how you can customize and navigate the Output window.

Tip 5.6: You can use F8 and Shift+F8 to navigate among errors in the Output window

F8 and Shift+F8 are bound to the commands *Edit.GoToNextLocation* and *Edit. GoToPreviousLocation*. If you have the Error List open, F8 and Shift+F8 take you directly to the error in question by highlighting that part of the code. If you have the Output window open, F8 and Shift+F8 put the cursor on each error listed.

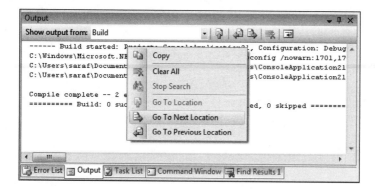

Tip 5.7: You can double-click messages in the Output window to jump to that location in the code

If you double-click any error or warning in the Output window, you jump directly to that location in the file or to the closest equivalent location.

There's also a button on the Output window toolbar that allows you to do the same thing, just in case you ever wondered what this Find Message In Code button did.

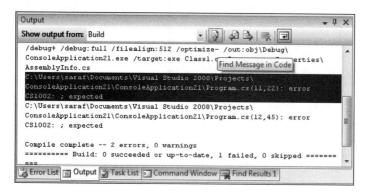

Tip 5.8: You can use the keyboard to jump to various panes within the Output window

The Output window has a Show Output From drop-down list, as shown in the following screen shot, to move between various outputs views (or panes), such as Debug and Build. There's a command called *Window.NextSubPane* that navigates to the next output pane.

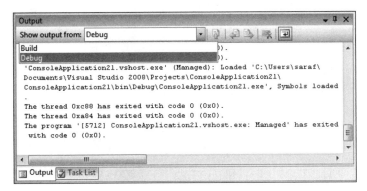

The command in itself isn't that interesting, but you can bind it to a keyboard shortcut—for example, Ctrl+Shift+Alt+O, since Ctrl+Alt+O is the keyboard shortcut to use for the Output window under the General Development Settings.

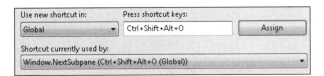

Now you can toggle easily between Debug and Build views in the Output window by using a keyboard shortcut.

Tip 5.9: How to stop the Output window from showing itself during a build

At some point, you'll experience the Output window sliding out from its autohiding place during a build. If you want to fine-tune this experience so that the Output window shows only when you tell it to (maybe you just want to check the status bar for the build status or have the Error List pop up if errors occur), go to Tools–Options–Projects And Solutions–General. Check the option called Show Output Window When Build Starts.

☑ Show Output window when build starts

Now the Output window will be displayed whenever a build is started.

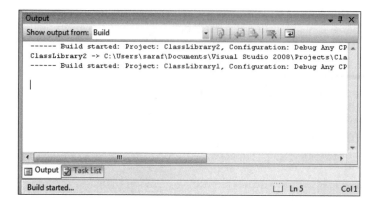

Tip 5.10: You can enable word wrap in the Output window

The Output window has an icon on the toolbar that allows you to enable word wrap.

> **Sara Aside** I don't use word wrap, as I prefer one line per error. But I see the potential if you have customized the Output window for space and need to read the entire line without having to scroll left or right.

Here is the Output window before pressing the Toggle Word Wrap button.

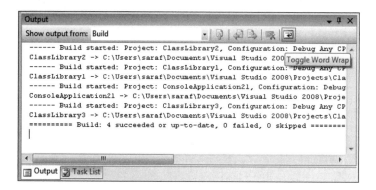

Here is the Output window after pressing the Toggle Word Wrap button.

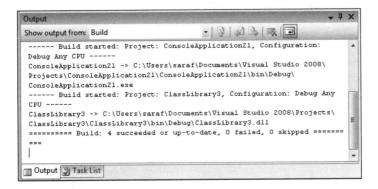

Tip 5.11: You can customize the color scheme in the Output window

On the Tools–Options–Environment–Fonts And Colors page, in the Show Settings For combo box, there's an Output Window option.

When it's selected, you'll be able to customize the colors for the following types of text: Plain Text, Selected Text, and Inactive Selected Text. Additionally, you can customize the color of the Current List Location.

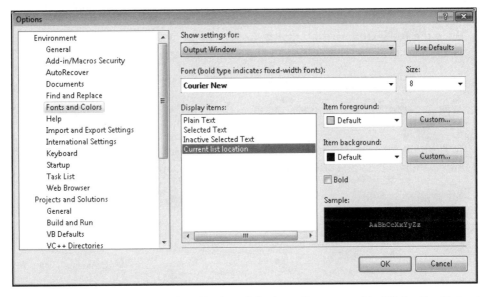

If you set the Item Background to Black and the Item Foreground to White, the Output window displays the visited line in the new color scheme.

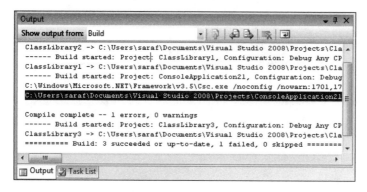

> **Sara Aside** For me, the dark blue has always been a bit distracting because it makes me think
> that the focus is in the Output window when it really is in the editor. Another good combination
> is to change Item Foreground to Cyan and Item Background to White.

Tip 5.12: You can redirect debug messages to the Output window

Depending on your environment settings, such as the Visual Basic Development Settings, you
may have noticed that the Output window's debug content is redirected to the Immediate
Window instead. Or maybe you want the Output window's debug content to go to the
Immediate Window.

Go to the Tools–Options–Debugging–General page. On this page, you'll find the option
Redirect All Output Window Text To The Immediate Window.

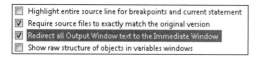

To illustrate, let's say you have this option enabled and you hit an assert. You'll see the assert
information in the Immediate Window and not in the Output window.

Tip 5.13: You cannot enable Stop Search on the Output window

> **Sara Aside** You may have noticed the Stop Search command on the Output window context menu. I spent a good 20 minutes trying to figure out how to enable this command before I broke down and e-mailed the developer.

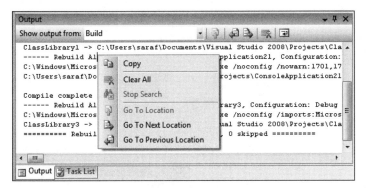

Apparently, you can't enable it. It's because the Output window and the Find Results window share a lot of implementation, and it should have been hidden for the Output window case.

Toolbox

The Toolbox is your one-stop shop for everything you can put into a designer or editor. These tips explore the ins and outs of your Toolbox, including how to use that General tab to quickly store a block of code.

Tip 5.14: You can drag and drop code onto the Toolbox's General tab

This tip is especially helpful if you are going to write code in a presentation. Instead of having to type code in front of everyone, you can have it all typed up on the side, ready to go!

You've probably noticed the Toolbox General tab showing this information by default.

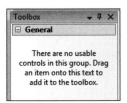

Probably one of the best-kept secrets is that you can actually drag and drop code onto the Toolbox. Just highlight some text and then Click+Drag and that text into the General tab. You'll see the following:

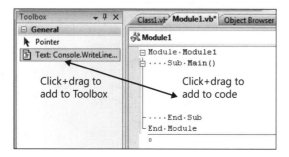

But it gets better.

You can actually drag code to any tab on the Toolbox, including user-created tabs. Note that you may need to select Show All on the Toolbox context menu to display additional tabs so that you can drag the code onto the tab. But after that, the tab will appear whenever you can insert code.

Tip 5.15: Why does each Toolbox group have a Pointer control?

You've probably noticed how the Pointer control appears at the top of each tab group. This is because whenever a control is selected in the Toolbox, the mouse pointer automatically becomes a drag pointer for that control, meaning that you just have to put your mouse pointer onto the form and click, and the control is dropped. You don't have to hold down any keys to do the actual drag.

But you may not actually want to use the drop function at this time. You can put the focus on the Pointer control to ensure that you don't accidentally drop the item.

Tip 5.16: How to stop the Toolbox from autopopulating with items found in the solution

Sara Aside The idea for this tip came from a blog reader. I'll admit that I didn't know how to keep the Toolbox from autopopulating. Fortunately, I can ask the developer on the feature directly and share the answer with everyone.

If you have a solution with lots of projects in it, and you notice the Toolbox is taking a long time scanning the solution for all possible Toolbox items, you can go to Tools–Options–Windows Forms Designer–General and set AutoToolboxPopulate to False.

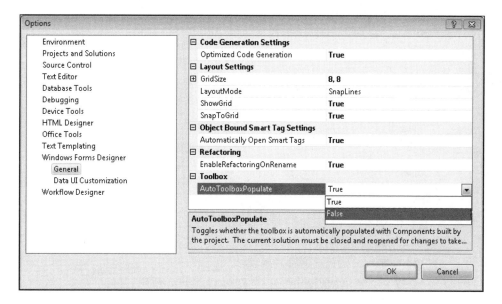

Tip 5.17: You can use * to expand all and / to collapse all in the Toolbox

> **Sara Aside** These keystrokes are not actually specific to the Toolbox, as they work for any standard TreeView control. I just call them out in the Toolbox because this is where I first discovered the * (asterisk) and / (forward slash) in our test-case repository.

Typing ***** expands everything in the Toolbox. Typing **/** collapses everything. (Just type the **/** key; do not use Shift+/ because that will produce a ?.)

Note that the * really does *expand all items, including subnodes*. In other words, I must warn you: *do not*, and I really mean *do not*, try to do this at your root c:\ directory. If you do, you'll get to watch Windows Explorer expand every single folder on your machine, which may take a while.

You can also consider using + (plus sign) and - (hyphen), which work for all standard TreeView controls without expanding all or collapsing all. I just tend to use the standard Right Arrow key to expand and Left Arrow key to collapse so that I don't have to reach as far.

To recap, typing ***** or **+** or pressing the Right Arrow key expands the tab.

And pressing **/** or **-** or pressing the Left Arrow key collapses the tab.

Tip 5.18: You can use Ctrl+Up Arrow and Ctrl+Down Arrow to move among the various control groups in the Toolbox

You could page up and down throughout the Toolbox to reach the previous or next control group, or you could just use Ctrl+Up Arrow or Ctrl+Down Arrow.

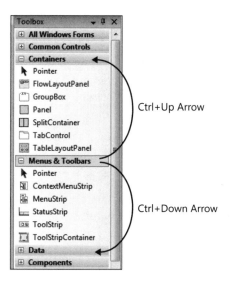

Tip 5.19: You can sort items in the Toolbox alphabetically

Most of the time, the controls are listed in alphabetical order. But if you ever need to do a reset, you can bring up the Toolbox context menu and select Sort Items Alphabetically.

Tip 5.20: You can switch between the Icon view and List Item view in the Toolbox

Here's yet another action I had no idea you could use until someone showed it to me. By having just the Icon view open, you can save a lot of space within the Toolbox.

For each Toolbox grouping, you can customize whether to show the flat list of controls and their names or just show their icons. Right-click anywhere in the desired group, and toggle off List View.

Here's the Icon view that appears instead of the List View.

Tip 5.21: You can use Show All to find your hiding Toolbox controls

> **Sara Aside**   This tip comes directly from the developer who works on the Toolbox. He told me he sees a lot of questions where people are trying to figure out why a particular control isn't there, especially when they've just recently added controls.

What happens is that all the controls in the Toolbox are managed by the active designer. A designer is like an editor because it takes up the same region of space in the IDE, but it allows you to design UI rather than write code. You can recognize a designer by the *[Design]* in the file tab. So, if the currently active designer doesn't support a particular control, you won't see it when you add it to the Toolbox.

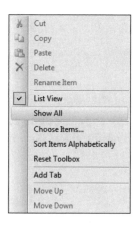

By choosing Show All, you can at least verify that your control was added. Now, how to get it active depends on the control and which designer is needed.

In the next screen shot, notice the scroll bar position on the right, showing just how many controls are now visible.

Tip 5.22: You can use Ctrl+C to copy controls in a Toolbox tab and then use Ctrl+V to paste the controls into another Toolbox tab

You can use the mouse to drag and drop controls to a new tab, and you can even use Ctrl+Drag to copy controls to a new tab. But did you know you can use the keyboard to achieve the same functionality?

Use the classic Ctrl+C to copy any Toolbox control, and use the classic Ctrl+V to paste into the desired tab location.

Note how the preceding image illustrates having both code and a button control within the General tab. Also note that I have the Show All option enabled to show the disabled code because when I took this screen shot, the WinForms designer was the active document in the IDE.

Tip 5.23: You can create new Toolbox tabs

You can create your own Toolbox tabs to store practically whatever you want in them. For that upcoming presentation, you can create your own tab by choosing the Add tab on the Toolbox context menu and adding content by using either the mouse or keyboard to populate content into your new tab. (Yes, the keyboard works too for cutting and pasting code from the editor into the Toolbox.)

> **Sara Aside**   I was going to create another tip called "Did you know you can move tabs?" but it doesn't really stand on its own as a separate tip. As I'm writing this, I still have three hours of battery life left for this plane flight, and the plane attendant people (I can't spell what they are called, and my row-seat neighbors are tired of playing human dictionary for me) just served brownies.

You can drag and drop Toolbox tabs to new locations in the list, and their location will persist.

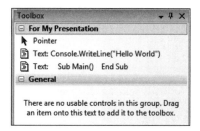

Task List

The Task List is similar to the Bookmarks window, where you can leave notes about particular sections of code. However, the Task List generates its content from scanning the source code files. For example, suppose you have left TODO comments in the code for others on your team to look at or as reminders the next time you check out that file. These TODO comments will appear in the Task List. Note that the user tasks and shortcuts created in the Task List are not inserted into the code, so these will remain for your eyes only.

Tip 5.24: You can use the Task List to create user tasks that are separate from your code

A user task is saved in the .suo file per user, unlike a TODO, HACK, or UNDONE comment that you type into your source code. A .suo file stores all of a user's solution customizations, which you wouldn't want checked into source control.

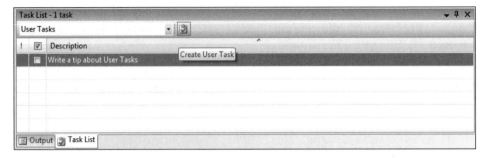

To create a user task, open View–Task List, make sure User Tasks is displayed in the combo box drop-down list, and then click the Create User Task button on the toolbar. Note that you can create the first task by directly editing the first row in the task list, but after that you need to press the button.

Then, as you finish your task, you can check the check box next to it to scratch it off.

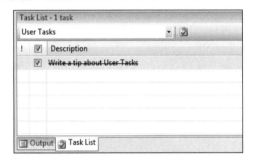

And to delete a task, simply right-click it and choose Delete.

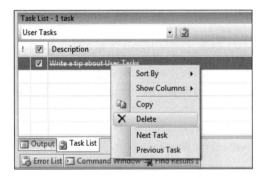

Tip 5.25: You can assign a priority to your Task List's user tasks

Now that you've created a user task, you can assign a priority. I call this out as a separate tip, as it is most likely not intuitive that you can do this.

Under the ! (exclamation point) column, you can click any cell to pop open the priority combo box.

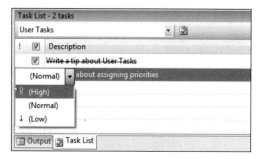

Then you'll be able to view and sort your user tasks based on priority.

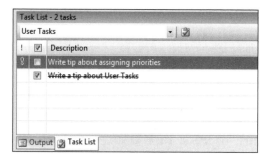

Tip 5.26: How to create and view TODO comments in the Task List

Let's focus now on the other aspect of the Task List: the comments left in the code. You need to drop down the combo box at the top right to show Comments to be able to see your comment tokens (for example, UNDONE, TODO, and HACKS) in the Task List.

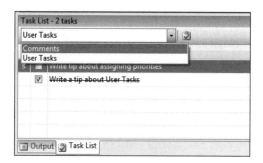

So let's say that you have a TODO comment in your code as shown here.

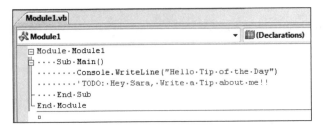

By going to the Comments view in the Task List, you can now see your TODO comment.

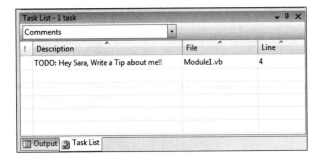

Tip 5.27: You can create shortcuts in your Task List

Sara Aide This is yet another feature I didn't know about until someone showed me.

You can store shortcuts in your Task List, and you can even use them as tasks to scratch off, if you want. And just like user tasks, shortcuts are saved in your solution .suo file, so they won't get checked into the source control.

To create a Task List shortcut, go to the desired location in your editor (which can be any line of code or comment) and then go to Edit–Bookmarks–Add Task List Shortcut.

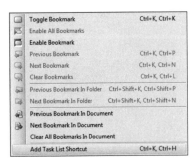

Now you'll notice the shortcuts curved-arrow glyph appears in the indicator margin.

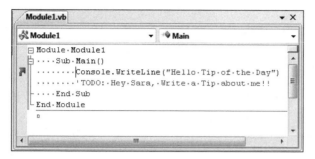

And now in the Task List, you'll see a new category called Shortcuts.

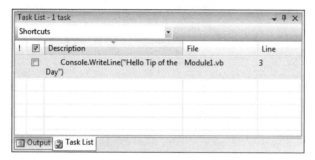

As illustrated in the preceding screen shot, you can also rename these shortcuts by double-clicking the description (or tabbing to the description field, for keyboard users) and then typing a new name.

> **Sara Aside** You may be wondering what the difference is between bookmarks and Task List shortcuts. At a high level, you won't see much difference. But, at the feature level, Task List shortcuts provide a few differences. Task List shortcuts display the entire line of code in the Task List window. Also, you can set a priority and check off these shortcuts as you complete them.

Tip 5.28: You can show HACK, UNDONE, and custom tokens in the Task List

TODO comments are not the only thing you can display under Comments in the Task List. If you go to Tools–Options–Environment–Task List, you'll see a Token List. By default, the Token List comes with HACK, UNDONE, and TODO, but you can create your own.

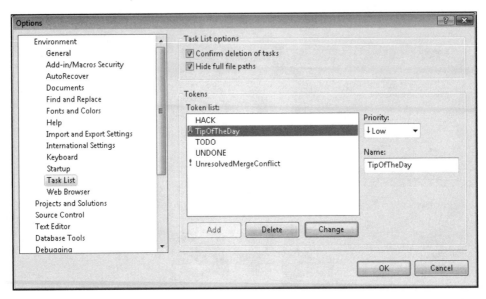

Using a user-created TipOfTheDay token, I can type a comment in my code using the 'TipOfTheDay token format, as shown here:

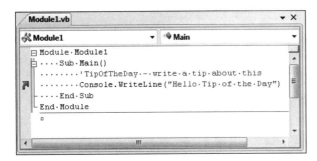

The TipOfTheDay comment now appears in the Task List.

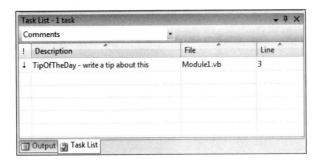

Tip 5.29: How to disable the prompt for deleting the Task List's user tasks

If you've created a few tasks and deleted them over time, you may have found that delete confirmation prompt to be annoying. Here's how you can disable it.

On each user task, you'll see the Delete command on the context menu, as shown in the following screen shot.

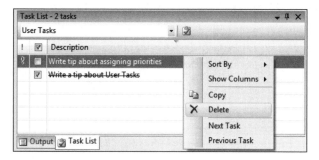

And when you click it, you'll get this prompt:

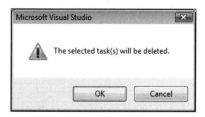

To disable this prompt, go to Tools–Options–Environment–Task List, and uncheck the Confirm Deletion Of Tasks check box.

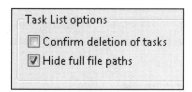

Tip 5.30: You can show a full file path in the Task List

This tip applies only to comments and shortcuts, as user tasks are not saved with a file.

Go to Tools–Options–Environment–Task List, and uncheck the Hide Full File Paths check box.

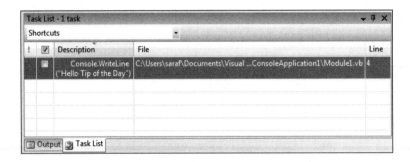

And now the Task List displays the full paths for shortcuts.

!	☑	Description	File	Line
	☐	Console.WriteLine ("Hello Tip of the Day")	C:\Users\saraf\Documents\Visual ...ConsoleApplication1\Module1.vb	4

Task List - 1 task
Shortcuts

Output   Task List

Tip 5.31: You can create keyboard shortcuts to navigate among the various Task List categories (by using *View.NextTask* and *View. PreviousTask*)

F8 and Shift+F8 are bound to the commands *Edit.GoToNextLocation* and *Edit. GoToPreviousLocation*. When the Task List is visible, these keyboard shortcuts navigate throughout all the tasks listed in a given category.

However, if you want to navigate at any time among your various TODO comments or other tasks, regardless of whether the Task List is open, the Task List comes with two commands for doing this: *View.NextTask* and *View.PreviousTask*.

Because we've already explored more than you ever wanted to know about the Task List, you now know that the Task List has several categories: User Tasks, Comments, and Shortcuts. These commands navigate only among items of a given category, so you won't jump from Shortcuts to User Tasks.

Note that these commands are not bound to a keyboard shortcut by default in the General Development Settings, so you may need to bind them yourself, depending on your development settings.

Shortcuts for selected command:
Ctrl+Alt+N (Global)   Remove

Use new shortcut in: Press shortcut keys:
Global   Ctrl+Alt+N   Assign

Shortcut currently used by:
View.NextTask (Ctrl+Alt+N (Global))

Go to Tools–Options–Environment–Keyboard, and in the Show Commands Containing edit box, type the command **View.NextTask**.

Do a sanity check for whether the settings you are using already have the command bound to a keyboard shortcut. If a command is already bound to a keyboard shortcut, you'll see it in the Shortcut Currently Used By read-only combo box, which you can see in the preceding screen shot.

If the command is not bound to a shortcut, in the Press Shortcut Keys edit box, type your preferred shortcut and click Assign. If you want this command to work only in the editor and not anywhere else in the IDE, use the Text Editor scope under the Use New Shortcut In drop-down list.

Rinse and repeat for the *View.PreviousTask* command. For me, I used Ctrl+Alt+N, only because it wasn't bound to anything in the General Development Settings. For the previous action, I highly recommend just adding the Shift key to whatever key combination you come up with for *View.NextTask*, since the standard convention for any backward navigation is to include Shift.

Also, something else to note, because we had to test for it, is that the Visual Studio status bar will update with the name of the comment when you use *View.NextTask* or *View.PreviousTask*.

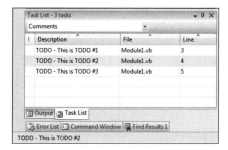

Object Browser

The Object Browser is your bird's-eye view on every possible object or method the IDE knows about, whether it lives in your project or in the Microsoft .NET Framework.

Tip 5.32: You can use Ctrl+Alt+J to open the Object Browser window

You can use Ctrl+Alt+J to open the Object Browser window. The command is *View.ObjectBrowser*.

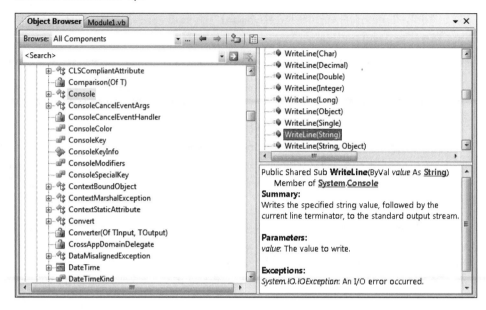

Tip 5.33: You can specify to show components in your solution only in the Object Browser

By default, the Object Browser shows you all the components in the latest .NET Framework version. But sometimes you don't need to know about the entire world, and you just want to focus on the objects in your solution.

In the upper-right corner of the Object Browser, you'll see a Browse combo box. If you drop down the combo box list, you'll see the option for selecting My Solution.

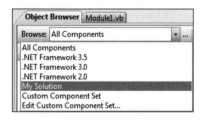

Now you'll see only the objects being used within your solution.

Tip 5.34: You can create a custom list of components for the Object Browser

You can create a custom components list for the Object Browser.

There are two ways to reach the Edit Custom Component Set dialog box. Either click that little "..." browse button next to the combo box or click the Edit Custom Component Set option in the Browse combo box.

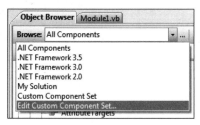

Now you'll see the Edit Custom Component Set window, where you can add and remove components. And for old time's sake, I've added an *Accessibility* assembly.

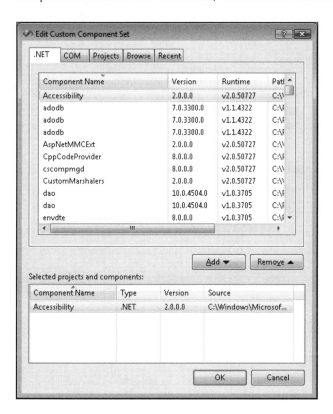

Finally, when returning to the Object Browser, you get the following view.

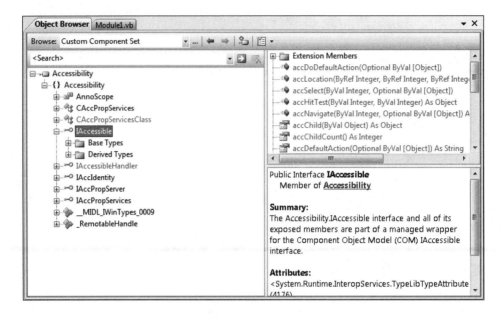

Tip 5.35: You can add references to your solution directly from the Object Browser

Let's say that you find the component that you want to add to your solution. Typically, you go to Solution Explorer, right-click the project node and select Add References, bring up the Add Reference dialog box, and you know how the rest goes.

Within the Object Browser, there's a toolbar button called Add To References located to the right of the "..." browse button and the forward/back navigation buttons.

With the *Accessibility* assembly selected, click the Add To References In Selected Project In Solution Explorer icon to add the assembly.

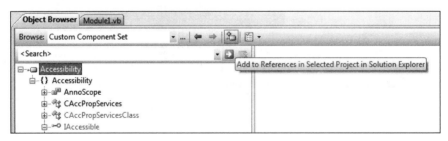

And now you'll see the *Accessibility* assembly added to the project.

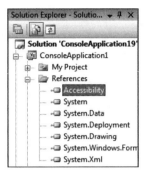

Tip 5.36: How to use navigate forward and back in the Object Browser

Another set of buttons on the Object Browser toolbar belongs to the Navigate Forward and Navigate Back actions.

The pages you visit within the Object Browser are saved in MRU (most-recently used) order.

This alone is somewhat exciting, but what really makes it exciting is a keyboard shortcut!

The commands are *View.ObjectBrowserForward* and *View.ObjectBrowserBack*. If you are using the Visual Basic Development Settings, you'll see that the keyboard shortcuts are Alt+Minus for Back and Shift+Alt+Minus for Forward. If you use the Forward and Back functionality frequently and are not using the Visual Basic Settings, go to Tools–Options–Environment–Keyboard, and manually set the keyboard shortcuts there.

Tip 5.37: You can create a keyboard shortcut for adding references to a solution from the Object Browser

> **Sara Aside** I was kind of surprised to see it in the list of commands. But, then again, one can never have too many keyboard shortcuts. =)
>
> To write this tip, I bound it to my pseudo random keyboard shortcut Ctrl+Alt+Shift+T. This is my generic, all-purpose keyboard shortcut that I use for testing purposes.

As far as binding *View.ObjectBrowserAddReference* to a keyboard shortcut goes, I'll leave it up to you to decide how useful this is. Maybe the "keyboard shortcut for everything" users will enjoy it.

As long as some object has selection—meaning it doesn't have to have focus (blue highlight) and has at least inactive selection (light gray highlight)—in the Objects pane (the leftmost pane), you'll get the following message box when you press the keyboard shortcut.

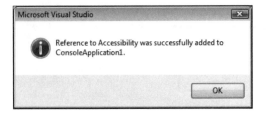

And if there's nothing selected (meaning you probably have absolutely nothing in the Object Browser) and you press the keyboard shortcut, Visual Studio will just stare at you.

Tip 5.38: You can customize both your Object pane and Members pane in the Object Browser

Over the next several tips, we're going to take apart the Object Browser Settings menu that lists what appears in the Object Browser.

The first set of options control your view preference in the Object pane, which is either by namespace or by containers. Think of these two options as a set of radio buttons that are mutually exclusive. The rest of the options are more like check boxes, since you can have all the show options enabled.

If you choose View Namespaces (which is the default), all components are shown based on their namespace, just as you would expect. The idea here is that namespaces stored in multiple physical containers are merged, as shown here:

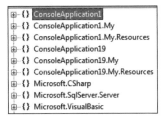

Now if you switch to View Containers, you'll see the physical containers, and then a breakdown of the namespaces that are contained in each.

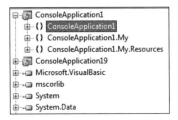

> **Sara Aside**   I always use View Containers so that I don't feel so overwhelmed by seeing everything! =)

Tip 5.39: You can choose whether to show base types in the Object Browser

In the Object Browser Settings menu, there's the Show Base Types option.

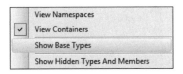

In the following example, *Class1* inherits from *ClassBase*. When this option is enabled, under *Class1* you'll see the Base Types folder. If you've been wondering how to get rid of this (or have been wondering how to enable it), just toggle the setting.

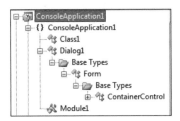

Tip 5.40: You can hide or show hidden members and types in the Object Browser

> **Sara Aside** I never officially tested the Object Browser but rather played back-up tester in case someone went on vacation, needed help analyzing failures during a full test pass, and so forth. When I wrote most of these tips, I had to browse the test cases and the documentation to make sure I described things consistently and to make sure I was not missing any functionality.

This tip is about the Show Hidden Types And Members option on the Object Browser Settings menu.

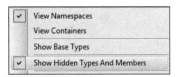

When this option is enabled, any hidden types and members will appear, but they'll appear in a grayed-out state, as shown next in the *Method1()* and *Method2()* example, where *Method2()* is hidden.

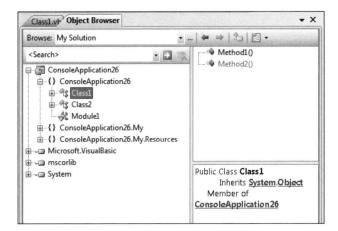

Tip 5.41: You can mark methods and types as Hidden so that they don't appear in Microsoft IntelliSense or in the Object Browser

Continuing from Tip 5.40, this tip is how to actually make something hidden or capable of being hidden.

In the *System.ComponentModel* namespace, there's the *EditorBrowseableAttribute* class.

Going back to the previous tip's *Method1()* and *Method2()* methods, you'll see in the following example how *Method2()* doesn't appear in IntelliSense, just like it doesn't appear in the Object Browser.

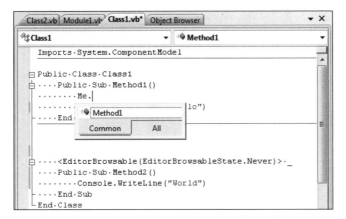

Of course, you can still complete the line just shown with *Method2()*, and everything will compile successfully.

Tip 5.42: What does *Other* mean in Show Other Members in Object Browser Settings?

The *Other* in the Show Other Members option represents members that do not have an access level of public, private, protected, or inherited. For example, access levels of *Friend* (in Visual Basic) and *Internal* (C#) fit into this *Other* category.

The Object Browser shows the *Friend* method with a blue diamond.

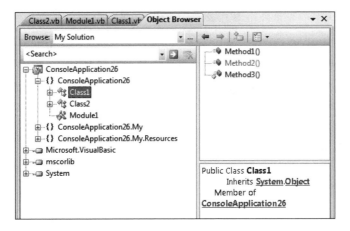

Tip 5.43: How to stop displaying all inherited members in the Object Browser Member pane

The next option in Object Browser Settings is Show Inherited Members.

When this option is enabled, you'll see all inherited members, including those inherited from *System.Object.*

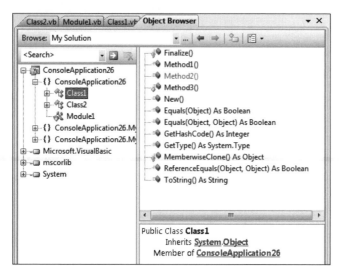

When this option is disabled, you'll see only *Method1()*, *Method2()*, and *Method3()*.

Tip 5.44: You can show extension methods in the Object Browser

This tip is new for Visual Studio 2008. You can learn more about extension methods in the documentation located at http://msdn.microsoft.com/en-us/library/bb384936.aspx *for Visual Basic and* http://msdn.microsoft.com/en-us/library/bb383977.aspx *for C#.*

In Object Browser Settings, you'll see the Show Extension Methods option.

Now, when you have an extension method in your code (in my example, it's a module because I'm using Visual Basic), you'll see a downward-pointing arrow.

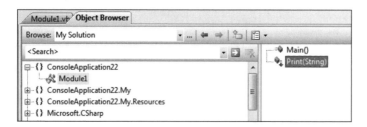

Tip 5.45: What are the two primary means of searching for objects in the Object Browser?

Now we'll move to the second toolbar in the Object Browser, which is all about searching.

The search scope depends on what you have selected in the Object Browser Scope. For example, if you try to search for System.Web in a Console Application, you will not be very successful.

There's also another way to search—it's using the Find And Replace window's Find Symbol functionality. You'll notice the Find Symbol search closely resembles the Object Browser search functionality.

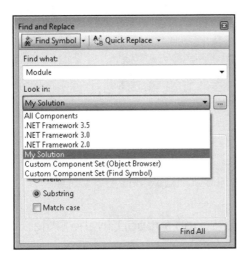

Tip 5.46: You can use F12 in the Object Browser to go to the definition of whatever is selected

On the context menu of both the Member pane (right panel) and the Object pane (left panel), you'll see the Go To Definition command. You can use this command to navigate directly into the code where whatever you have selected is defined (or you'll get a nice error message).

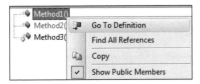

The *Edit.GoToDefinition* command is bound to F12. Pressing F12 in the image just shown takes you to where *Method1()* is defined in the code.

Tip 5.47: You can use a Find Symbol search (Shift+F12) in the Object Browser

Just like the previous tip that talked about going to an object's or function's definition, you can find all the references of what you have selected in the Object Browser.

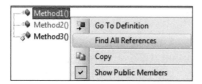

The command *Edit.FindAllReferences* is bound to Shift+F12. When you press Shift+F12, it brings up the Find All References window.

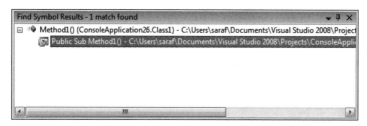

This is the same as using Find Symbol in the Find In Files window.

Tip 5.48: How to use type-ahead selection support in the Object Browser

You may have tried this tip on your own, just hoping it would work. But in case you never thought about it, the Object Browser supports type-ahead selection.

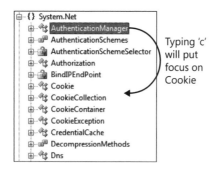

Sara Aside Back in the Visual Studio .NET 2003 days, I was on a quest for a while to have all lists in the IDE support type-ahead selection. I did what I could, so if you see a list that should support it and it doesn't, definitely file a bug with the Visual Studio Team. Maybe one day my quest will be completed.

Tip 5.49: You can export all your Object Browser customizations in a .vssettings file

Over these past several tips, we've taken a close look at customizing your Object Browser experience, from sorting to searching to filtering, among other options.

Your customizations can be saved to a .vssettings file via the Tools–Import And Export Settings dialog page, under General Settings–Object Browser Options.

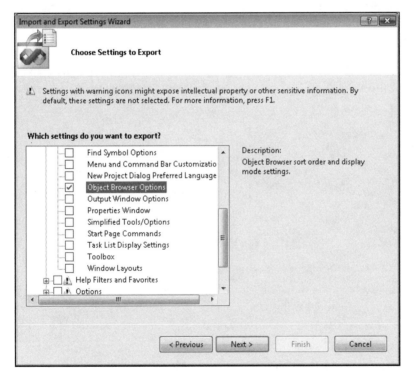

The good news is that the XML stored in the created .vssettings file for the Object Browser Settings is human readable, in case you need to make a quick tweak.

Tip 5.50: Why the Object Browser has so many commands you can bind to (and how to create a keyboard shortcut to clear the search results)

> **Sara Aside** As I've been writing the Object Browser tip series, I have noticed that there are *a lot* of commands available under Tools–Options–Environment–Keyboard. Just type **ObjectBrowser** and you'll see what I mean.

Technically, not all these commands need keyboard shortcuts. For example, the ability to sort objects by access level probably doesn't need a keyboard shortcut. But since they do have shortcuts, let's have some fun....

If you bind any of the Object Browser Settings options to a keyboard shortcut, you'll see that shortcut in the drop-down menu. I didn't know that until I started playing with this feature.

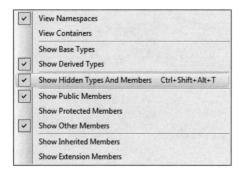

How can you take advantage of this? If you use the Object Browser a lot to search, you might find it meaningful to clear the search via the keyboard shortcut. The command *View. ObjectBrowserClearSearch* clears the search combo, thus clearing the Object Browser filter.

Tip 5.51: You can use the *View.Forward* (Alt+Right Arrow) and *View. Backward* (Alt+Left Arrow) global commands in the Object Browser

In Tip 5.36, I discussed how you can navigate forward and backward with the Alt+Minus and Shift+Alt+Minus keyboard shortcuts, which are scoped specifically to the Object Browser. But there are two other commands, *View.Forward* and *View.Backward,* that also work in the Object Browser, just like Alt+Minus and Shift+Alt+Minus.

View.Forward and *View.Backward* are *global*, meaning that other features within the IDE can use them. For example, Class View uses them in the same way as the Object Browser. But you're probably most familiar with these commands as Web Browser Forward and Web Browser Backward.

If you are accustomed to using these commands elsewhere in the IDE, you'll feel right at home in the Object Browser.

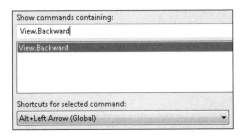

Chapter 6
Discover More Tools for Your Design Time, Part 2

In continuing to explore all the tools provided by the IDE, this chapter focuses on dialog boxes and smaller, miscellaneous tools in Microsoft Visual Studio. For example, you can have a lot of fun using the Find combo box to run Visual Studio commands, open files, and much more. There are all sorts of tips and tricks here that, even if you don't use them in your daily coding activities, you can definitely use to impress your coworkers with your mad IDE skills.

Dialog Boxes

Unlike tool windows, which are available at any time, dialog boxes are used when a tool needs to perform some sort of action that can't or shouldn't be interrupted. For example, resetting your development settings requires a series of actions that should be done at one time, such as choosing which settings you want to reset to and deciding whether you want to save your current settings. These actions are best handled through a dialog box that walks you through each step instead of a tool window, where you may come back and say, "Hmm, what was I doing again?"

Conversely, having to open a dialog box every time you want to drag and drop a control onto a WinForm designer would get very old very quickly. Because the Toolbox is a tool window and not a dialog box, it can live alongside your WinForm designer for easy access.

Import And Export Settings

The Import And Export Settings feature was the first feature I ever tested from start to finish, from watching the specification get written to shipping the feature in the beta release of Visual Studio 2005. The Import And Export Settings dialog box will always be near and dear to my heart.

The code name for the feature was Profiles. Some of the earliest check-ins even referred to the feature as such in the UI. Something definitely got hard-wired in my head, because I always slip and call the feature Profiles whenever I talk about it. My efforts to deprogram myself have not been successful.

Tip 6.1: How to find what development settings you last reset to

Maybe you don't remember what you picked during your first launch of Visual Studio or what you last reset to.

Under the HKEY_CURRENT_USER\Software\Microsoft\VisualStudio\9.0\Profile key, you'll see the *LastResetSettingsFile* value. As previously mentioned, the code name for this feature was Profiles, hence the word *Profile* is used as the key.

In the following example, you'll notice how I'm using the General Development Settings.

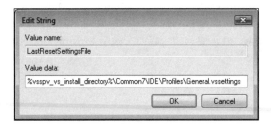

If you haven't reset any settings since launching Visual Studio, this value tells you this is what you picked at first launch.

Tip 6.2: How to reset your environment settings via Tools–Import And Export Settings

The most popular question I see about Visual Studio IDE is how to reset the environment settings. Starting in Visual Studio 2005, the IDE prompts you on first launch to pick your development settings. If you need to reset back to what you picked or want to pick previously saved settings or predefined settings, go to Tools–Import And Export Settings to launch the wizard, and choose Reset All Settings.

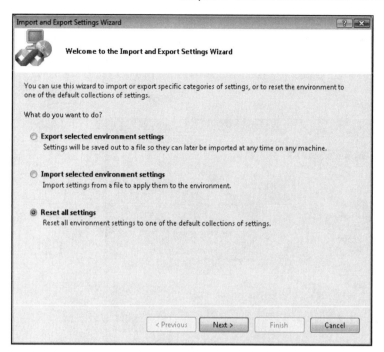

On the next page you decide whether you want to save your current settings. If this is your first time using this dialog box or you want to experiment with this feature, or both, definitely choose to save your settings. The default is to save your settings, so go with the default if you are unsure.

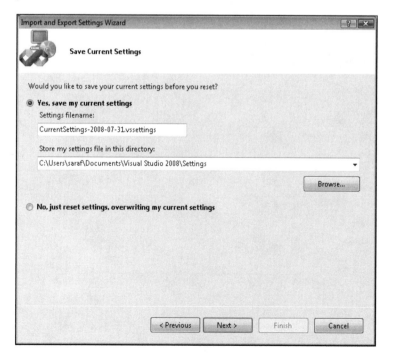

The following page is much more interesting. You may notice this list looks familiar. It should, because this is the same list from that first launch dialog box that prompts you to pick your preferred environment settings. These files contain default settings for features such as keyboard shortcut bindings, tool window layouts, project template layouts, and many, many more.

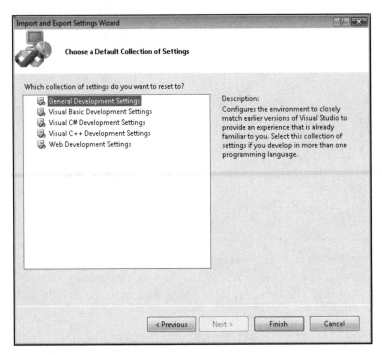

Choose your IDE settings by clicking Finish. Visual Studio lets you know whether any issues arose with regard to resetting your settings.

Tip 6.3: What settings are contained in the New Project Dialog Preferred Language category

If you go to Tools–Import And Export Settings–Export Settings, you'll see the list of categories that can be contained in a .vssettings file. The first category I want to discuss is the New Project Dialog Preferred Language category.

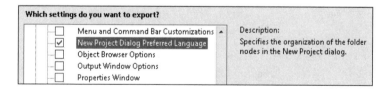

As noted in the description, it organizes the New Project Dialog folders based on the preferred language. If C# is preferred, all the C# projects are listed at the top of the list and all the others are collected toward the bottom.

The General Development Settings use the defaults that have been familiar since the Visual Studio .NET 2002 days, as shown here:

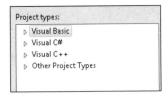

Now let's see the dialog box using the Visual C# Development Settings. Note how Visual Basic and Visual C++ fall into the newly created Other Languages node.

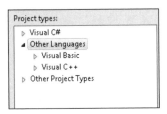

Tip 6.4: You can add your own files to the Import And Export Settings–Reset page list

If you go to the Reset page on the Tools–Import And Export Settings Wizard, you'll see the list of files you can reset to. These settings files are the ones created by the Visual Studio team. But, let's say that one of the default files has some small option that just annoys you or you want to add your own file to the list, as shown here:

These files live at \Program Files\Microsoft Visual Studio 9.0\Common7\IDE\Profiles. You'll need administrator rights to access Program Files, so please use this tip at your own risk.

In this folder, you can add your own .vssettings files or modify the existing ones. I use the General Development Settings, but any time I do a reset, the Tools–Customize–Show Shortcut Keys In ScreenTips option becomes unchecked. This option shows you the keyboard shortcut for a toolbar button in the ToolTip, a visual cue I absolutely must have.

If you find yourself in a similar situation, where you want to make small tweaks to one of the default settings files provided, you can do the following:

1. Reset to General Development Settings.

2. Enable the setting or settings you prefer.

3. Do a full export (for example, check all options in the Export page), and write over the General Development Settings.

4. Copy this file over the existing General Development Settings file that lives in \Program Files.

The next time you reset using these settings, you'll see your preferred settings. And in my case, I'll see my keyboard shortcuts in my ToolTips!

Tip 6.5: What's the difference between resetting settings and importing settings?

Whenever I demo Tools–Import And Export Settings, I'm usually asked to explain the difference between the Import feature and the Reset feature.

From an end-user perspective, importing everything in that particular settings file provides the same functionally as a reset.

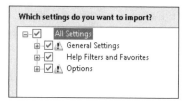

But of course, there's more going on under the UI surface. Whenever you do a reset, the IDE stores the path of the file you picked to reset to in the registry. There are some shortcuts within the IDE to quickly reset those settings. Following are a couple of the most common of these quick reset options.

First, on the Tools–Options–Environment–Fonts And Colors page, you'll see the Use Defaults option. This option resets your fonts and colors using the settings file you last reset to.

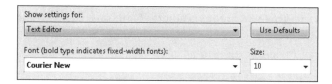

Second, on the Window menu, there's the command Reset Window Layout. This command resets your window layouts (that is, all your tool windows in all four window layout states) using the settings file you last reset to.

But ... What if you attempt to reset using a file you last reset to that didn't contain this particular category? For example, let's say you last reset to your own settings file and it didn't contain the Window Layouts category. Then I believe Visual Studio uses its *factory defaults* (the legacy settings that were built in for Visual Studio .NET 2003, the version before the Import And Export Settings feature was built) whenever you do Windows–Reset Window Layout. I recall during one of the many Profiles feature design meetings the term *schizophrenia* being used to describe the possible states Visual Studio could end up in. =D

Tip 6.6: You can save your current settings prior to doing an Import or Reset

Sara Aside Sometimes "Tip of the Day" isn't about stating the obvious; it's about stating the nonobvious. A lot of times, there's functionality that seems trivial on the surface, but one-off things occur at a deeper level, as seen in Tip 6.5. Fortunately, this tip is trivial. No hidden operations going on under the UI that I have to explain.

Whenever you do a destructive operation via Tools–Import And Export Settings, such as importing or resetting your settings, Visual Studio prompts you to save your current settings prior to continuing. This operation is the same as doing a full export (that is, going to the Export page and checking everything to export to a file).

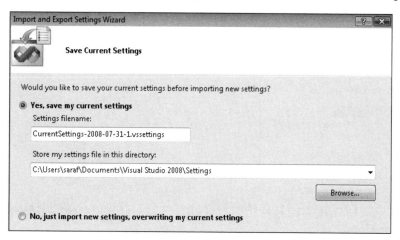

The one thing I'll call out is that the Store My Settings File In This Directory combo box will remember any location where you've exported a file to, because you may wish to save your current settings there again in the future.

Tip 6.7: How Visual Studio automatically saves all your current settings every time you close it

On the Tools–Options–Environment–Import And Export Settings (yes, the Tools–Import And Export Settings dialog box has its own Tools Options page), you'll find the option that lets you choose where to store your current settings. Note that you don't get to opt out of this. Prior to Visual Studio 2005, settings categories were saved in separate files in %appdata%, such as a file for all your toolbox customizations, your window layouts, your keyboard short-cut bindings, and your command bar changes. Starting in Visual Studio 2005, those settings are now stored in a centralized file called the CurrentSettings.vssettings file by default.

Every time Visual Studio shuts down, it writes to this file location to keep your current settings saved.

If you ever make a change that you need to quickly back out of, you can always go to Tools–Import And Export Settings–Import and choose the CurrentSettings.vssettings file, located in the My Settings folder.

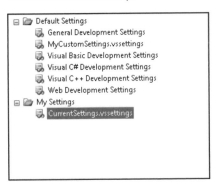

Tip 6.8: You can copy the full file path from the final wizard page when exporting settings

This tip is more like a "tip" than my usual "micro functionality" daily tips. After you export, the final page of the wizard shows you the full file path. This page is just a read-only edit box that can take focus. In other words, you can put your cursor in it and copy the full file path.

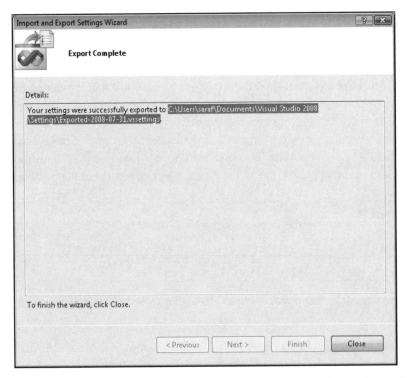

After you export your settings, you may want to open the file and see what's there, in case you want to make any tweaks. Otherwise, you'll have to open the Import And Export Settings dialog box and go through the wizard to guess where you exported that file to.

Tip 6.9: You can use team settings to keep Visual Studio settings on different machines in sync

Under Tools–Options–Environment–Import And Export Settings, you'll see an option called Use Team Settings File.

This option enables you to let all the members of your team use the same baseline settings. You can provide a .vssettings file (by creating these customizations on your machine and then using Tools–Import And Export Settings–Export to create the file). Then put the .vssettings file on a Universal Naming Convention (UNC) share. Next, you check the Use Team Settings File check box, pointing it at this file.

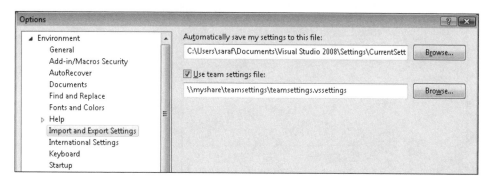

So, what happens now? Whenever Visual Studio launches, it'll check the time stamp of the .vssettings file, and if there has been an update, Visual Studio will reapply all the settings from the .vssettings file. But be aware, if you have any custom changes, they will be overwritten when Visual Studio detects the new team settings file.

I think that this works really well in a scenario where there's a single developer who works on multiple computers, because any tweaks the developer makes on one machine will be carried over to the next machine.

External Tools

The External Tools feature allows you to run tools that are not part of Visual Studio, such as good old notepad.exe, from within the IDE instead of having to launch the tool manually. For example, you can place a menu item to notepad.exe on the Tools menu and launch it instead of having to go to the actual location of the Notepad executable on disk.

Additionally, you can customize how these tools are launched, including providing arguments and writing information to the Output window. These tips explore what you can do with External Tools.

Tip 6.10: You can run external tools from the IDE

> **Sara Aside** Okay I have to admit, I'm not the local expert in External Tools. I can talk about the functionality all day long, but nothing is better than real-world examples. When I blogged about this tip, I asked blog readers to leave comments about how they use this feature. You can see their comments at *http://blogs.msdn.com/saraford/archive/2008/04/24/did-you-know-you-can-run-external-tools-within-visual-studio-201.aspx.*

Let's start with the basics. Go to Tools–External Tools to bring up the External Tools dialog box. You'll notice a set of built-in tools ready to go for you.

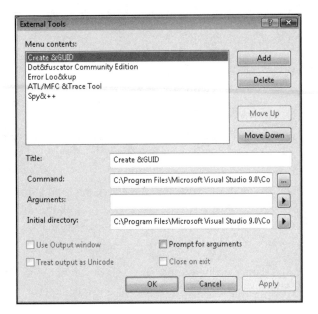

This list of tools under Menu Contents maps directly to the list presented on the Tools menu, as shown here:

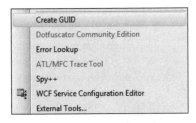

> **Sara Aside** The first time I made this connection I was totally taken aback. I probably saw this list of tools for years, but I never knew it came directly from the External Tools dialog box.

Tip 6.11: You can add your own external tools to the list

For this tip, let's add Notepad as an external tool.

Go to the Tools–External Tools dialog box, and you'll see the Add button. Click Add to create a [New Tools 1] placeholder. Rename the title by typing **Notepad**.

For the Command edit box, use the name of the actual executable. You should be able to just type **notepad.exe**, depending on your environment variables.

This is the minimum amount of information you need to include to make an external tool work. But let's go a little further by exploring the optional arguments.

For Arguments, you can type the name of a file, either an existing file if you want Notepad to open it or the name of a file if you want Notepad to create.

For Initial Directory, you can type the file path, either the path where the filre exists or where you want Notepad to create it.

And of course, you'll see Notepad now in the Tools menu.

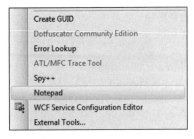

We'll explore more of the arguments and other options in the upcoming tips.

Tip 6.12: You can rearrange the list of external tools and create mnemonics

Continuing with the newly added Notepad tool from the previous tip, you can use the External Tools dialog box to sort your list of external tools as they will appear on the Tools menu. To the right of the Menu Contents list, you'll find the Move Up and Move Down buttons.

You can specify a mnemonic, also known as a keyboard accelerator, by putting an ampersand in front of the letter to be used as the accelerator in the Title field.

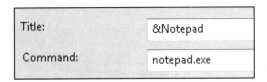

Now, on the Tools menu, you can simply press *n* to launch Notepad.

If there's a mnemonic conflict, the focus cycles among the commands that share that mnemonic. Then you press Enter at the appropriate command to execute the command. It is ideal to have no conflicts.

Tip 6.13: You can have your external tool's text displayed in the Output window

At the bottom of the External Tools dialog box, you'll see more options for customizing the external tool within the IDE. This tip is about the Use Output Window option. The idea here is you're running a .bat file and you want to track the progress within the IDE.

Using the command prompt as the tool, you can set Arguments to something like */C echo $(CurText)*, which signifies the following:

- */C*, from cmd.exe, carries out the command specified by the string and then terminates.

- *$(CurText)* is a token that comes from Visual Studio that represents the currently selected text, displayed as Current Text in the menu.

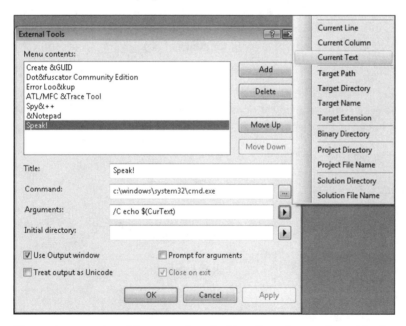

Now, when running this external tool with a line of text selected in the editor, the Output window displays the text.

```
Program.cs

ConsoleApplication36.Program                    ▼  Main(string[] args)

        using·System.Text;

      namespace·ConsoleApplication36
        {
          ····class·Program
          ····{
          ········static·void·Main(string[]·args)
          ········{
          ···········Console.WriteLine("Hi·from·ConsoleApplication36");
          ········}
          ····}
        }

Output

Show output from:  Speak!                  ▼  🗐 | 🗐 🗐 | 🗟 | 🔁

    "Console.WriteLine("Hi from ConsoleApplication36");"
    |
```

Tip 6.14: How the external tools tokens work

I've hinted at a few of the external tool tokens, but let's explore a little more. Most of these are self-explanatory and are explored in depth in the documentation, but here I'll give you a high-level overview. You can view the documentation at *http://msdn2.microsoft.com/en-us/library/ekbzk5f8.aspx*.

All Item and Current tokens that are available for the Arguments edit box operate on the currently active editor. Note the editor does not need to have focus to be able to work, but it must at least have inactive selection.

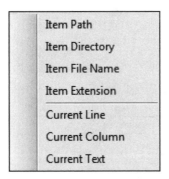

For the Initial Directory edit box, you'll find all the directory tokens, but one in particular to call out is the Binary Directory. Note the Binary Directory option is new for Visual Studio 2008.

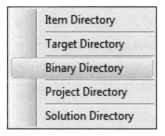

The Target Directory token targets the obj directory (\obj\Debug\), but if you need the final bits that go into the bin directory (\bin\Debug\), use the Binary Directory token.

Tip 6.15: You can prompt for arguments when you run an external tool

To finish the customization of the external tools, you can check Prompt For Arguments if you need to enter or edit values each time you run the tool.

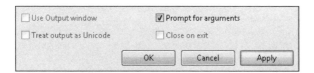

So now, if I need to specify which file I want Notepad to open, I'm prompted for the file name, which is the argument for notepad.exe.

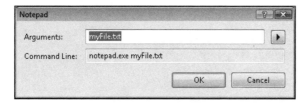

And recall that you can set the Initial Directory, where Notepad is going to look for files.

Find Combo Box

It wasn't until I took over testing the editor that I learned that the Find combo box runs Visual Studio commands. And it wasn't until I found Tip 6.16 that I learned that the Find combo box can combine keyboard shortcuts and command arguments.

I feel like this section is really a collection of tricks, as these tips truly embrace the spirit of "Did you know ...".

Find Combo Box Runs Commands

This section describes all the things you can do with the Find combo box to run commands, like getting help for a particular keyword, opening a file without any UI, or setting a breakpoint on a given function name.

Tip 6.16: How to have fun with the Find combo box

> **Sara Aside** I learned from our test cases that you can run commands via the Find combo box. But, when I found Shawn Farkas's blog (*http://blogs.msdn.com/shawnfa*), it took what I knew about the Find combo box to a whole new level.

Following are some examples of commands you can run from the Find combo box, but the idea is that many Visual Studio commands take parameters that you can enter into the Find combo box. Hit the keyboard shortcut to a Visual Studio command, and the command will pull its parameters from the Find combo box.

Press Ctrl+D to go to the Find combo box. Now here are a few ways you can have some fun:

- **Go to a line** Type the line number, and press Ctrl+G. I like showing this off as how you can do a "go to line" without popping up the Go To dialog box.

- **Go to a file** Type the name of the file (either in your project or on the INCLUDE path), and press Ctrl+Shift+G.

- **Get help** Type the keyword, and press F1.

You can also use command aliases, as shown here:

- To get a call stack, type >**kb**.

- To go to a Web page, type >**nav http://www.codeplex.com**.

You can read Shawn's full blog post at http://blogs.msdn.com/shawnfa/archive/2004/02/27/81338.aspx.

Tip 6.17: You can press Ctrl+/ to run Visual Studio commands in the Find combo box

> **Sara Aside** I had to do a little research to remember what this feature is called. I remember calling this feature the "command line" in our test cases. But, after some internal debates, I was told it is really just the Find combo box running commands. Regardless of what the feature is called, you can run Visual Studio commands without having to open the Command Window.

Press Ctrl+/ to reach the Find combo box; the ">" will be inserted for you. Of course, you could press Ctrl+D and then type **>** if you really wanted to.

It's like Microsoft IntelliSense, but for Visual Studio commands instead.

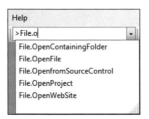

Note that you may need to use a different keyboard shortcut, depending on which environment settings you are using. If Ctrl+/ does not work for you, go to Tools–Options–Environment–Keyboard to see what keyboard shortcut the *Tools.GoToCommandLine* command is bound to.

Tip 6.18: How to open a file in the solution without using either a tool window or a dialog box

> **Sara Aside** A blog reader's question inspired this tip. I receive a lot of e-mail asking me how to do something in Visual Studio. The majority of the questions I don't have the answers to, as they are out of my scope of testing or beyond my experience. So I'm always excited and relieved to see a question that is within my scope, like this one in particular. When I saw the words, "keyboard shortcut" and "open a file," I knew I could give a meaningful reply.

The idea here is you just want to press some keyboard shortcut, type the file name that's in the solution, and go directly to that file. No Solution Explorer. No Open File dialog box. No UI.

Here we go …

1. Press Ctrl+/. This brings you the Find combo box with the ">" already included for you.

2. Type **File.OpenFile <*filename*>**. You'll notice support for autocompletion.

3. Select a file, and press Enter to open the file.

Because the command *File.OpenFile* seems to me to be very long to type, you can use the following steps to create an alias that is shorter:

1. Press Ctrl+/.
2. Type **alias fo File.OpenFile** to create a command alias.

Now, for the rest of time or until you reset your command aliases, you can:

1. Press Ctrl+/.
2. Type **fo** *<filename>*.

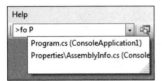

And now your file is opened in the editor. Tool windows and dialog boxes are not required.

Tip 6.19: You can set a breakpoint on a function from the Find combo box

In the standard command bar, you'll see the Find combo box right next to Find In Files. Obviously, you can type a function name and hit Enter to search, but where's the fun in that?

Type the name of the method, as I have in the preceding screen shot, and hit F9. You'll notice the breakpoint is set at function *Main*.

```
class Program
{
    static void Main(string[] args)
    {
    }
}
```

Why did this happen?

F9 is bound to a command called *Debug.ToggleBreakpoint*. If there's text in the Find combo box and you run a Visual Studio command from within the Find combo box, the IDE will use that text as the command parameter. In the case of F9, the IDE toggled a breakpoint at the specified function, hence setting a breakpoint at *Main()*.

Start Page

The Start Page provides a way to quickly open recent projects, links to information about how to get started, and the RSS feed. Technically, the Start Page is a tool window, so it is possible to dock it, float it on a secondary monitor, and so forth. But I've always seen it used in the center of the IDE. This is probably why I've always seen it documented internally as its own stand-alone feature, so I didn't see a need to change tradition.

Start Page Window

This section covers the tweaks you can make to the Start Page, including how to change the default RSS feed and how to prevent it from showing whenever you launch Visual Studio.

Tip 6.20: You can change the RSS feed on the Visual Studio Start Page

Go to Tools–Options–Environment–Startup and in the Start Page News Channel text box, you can change the current RSS feed to the desired RSS feed.

You can also update the time in minutes to pull content from the feed. Note that once you click OK on the Tools–Options dialog box, the RSS content will be pulled automatically.

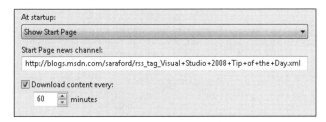

If you want to read the "Tip of the Day" series from your Start Page, here's the RSS feed to use:

http://blogs.msdn.com/saraford/rss_tag_Visual+Studio+2008+Tip+of+the+Day.xml

Tip 6.21: How to customize what Visual Studio opens to (or how to make the Start Page not show up when Visual Studio opens)

> **Sara Aside**   When I was working on either my test cases or the automation framework, I would use the Last Loaded Solution option. When I was doing ad hoc testing, just randomly testing for bugs, I would have either the Show Empty Environment or Show New Project Dialog Box option set.

Under Tools–Options–Environment–Startup, you'll find the At Startup combo box.

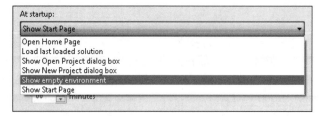

Following is a list of the items you can select to specify what you want Visual Studio to open to:

- Your Web browser home page. Note that the option to change your Web browser home page is found in Tools–Options–Environment–Web Browser.

- The last loaded solution.

- The Open Project dialog box.

- The New Project dialog box.

- Show Empty Environment. Choosing this option results in Visual Studio showing an empty environment without a document.

- The Start Page. This is the default setting.

Chapter 7
Know Your Solutions, and Other Project and Debugging Tweaks

All good things must come to an end.

Throughout the book, I've talked about having tested nearly every feature area of Microsoft Visual Studio, moving to a new area every six months or so. Testing the project and solution feature area completed my tour of the core IDE features. After four and a half years of testing Visual Studio by using the build of Visual Studio we were testing to write test code (yes, it is meant to be recursively confusing) and after three product cycles, I decided it was time to get up and stretch my program management skills. Shortly after Visual Studio 2005 launched, I moved to the Visual Studio Community Team as a program manager.

I definitely miss software testing. It was so much fun to be creative and break stuff. But then again, getting to spray-paint "Embrace Open Source on CodePlex" on your Microsoft office window is a pleasure that's right up there with "You broke it, and I'm telling."

Project and Solution System

You will always have a solution to contain your projects, even if you have only one project. The solution concept started in Visual Studio .NET 2002 as a way to support having one IDE for all the various languages. Following are some tips for interacting with both your project (or projects) and your solution.

Multitargeting

Prior to Visual Studio 2008, there was only one version of the Microsoft .NET Framework supported for any given version of the IDE. Multitargeting allows you to use the latest features in the Visual Studio 2008 IDE while providing the flexibility to choose which version of the .NET Framework to target.

Tip 7.1: How Visual Studio 2008 supports multitargeting of the .NET Framework

> **Sara Aside** This was the tip of the day for the official Visual Studio 2008 launch. I figured I needed to pick something huge about Visual Studio 2008 to talk about on this day.

A popular new feature for Visual Studio 2008 is the ability to multitarget the .NET Framework. This means that you can use the latest version of the IDE but still be able to target the .NET Framework 2.0 (or .NET Framework 3.0) as needed.

Scott Guthrie has an excellent write-up on multitargeting support on his blog at *http://weblogs.asp.net/scottgu/archive/2007/06/20/vs-2008-multi-targeting-support.aspx*.

Because Scott did his write-up in C#, I'll take a picture using Visual Basic. And apparently Scott knows about Tip 7.3. =)

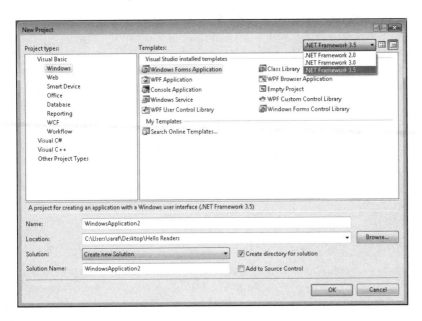

Projects

This section contains small tweaks for customizing your projects, ranging from using solution folders to hide your project to creating "throw away" projects that won't cause the ConsoleApplication57 phenomenon.

Tip 7.2: How to change the default new-project location

In the New Project dialog box, you can change the default new-project location.

The option to do so lives in Tools–Options–Projects And Solutions–General.

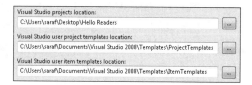

Tip 7.3: You can toggle between small icons and large icons in the New Project dialog box

Sara Aside It is amazing how many times I've pulled up the New Project dialog box in my lifetime and never noticed the Small/Large icon buttons in the upper-right corner.

Okay, be honest, how long have you been using Visual Studio and are just now noticing those icons for the first time? =) I had been on the Visual Studio team for an entire year before someone pointed them out to me. You learn something new every day.

Here's the New Project dialog box using small icons.

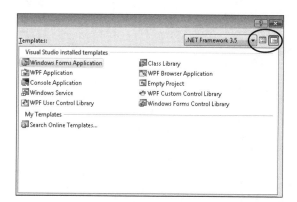

And here's the New Project dialog box using large icons.

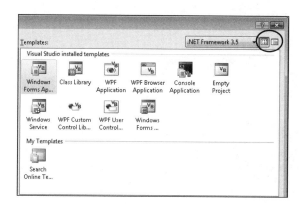

Tip 7.4: You can use solution folders to hide projects

In the Solution Explorer, you can group projects inside of solution folders to improve the manageability of solutions that contain a large number of projects.

With the focus on the Solution node in the Solution Explorer, the Add New Solution Folder button becomes available. Now you can drag projects into this solution folder, as shown next.

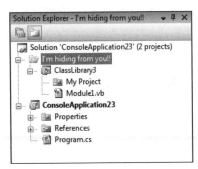

But let's actually hide the project. Right-click your newly created solution folder and choose Hide Folder. Now the project is hidden, and a new icon appears to unhide the projects. And yes, you can still build successfully in this state.

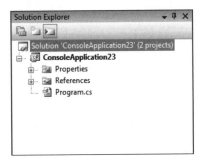

Tip 7.5: You can create temp or "throw away" projects

If you need to create small projects to try things out or you're not sure how you want to set up things *before* you save, there's an option for this.

Go to Tools–Options–Projects And Solutions–General, and uncheck the Save New Projects When Created check box.

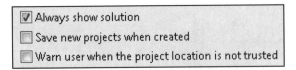

When this option is unchecked, the Location edit box and several others will be gone from the New Project dialog box.

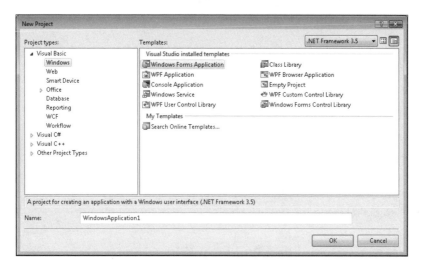

This tip is helpful to know in case you, like several readers who have contacted me, accidentally find yourself missing a few edit boxes.

Tip 7.6: How to hide or show the Project Location Is Not Trusted message box

When you attempt to open a project hosted on a Universal Naming Convention (UNC) share (for example, \\server\folder), you'll get the following warning message box.

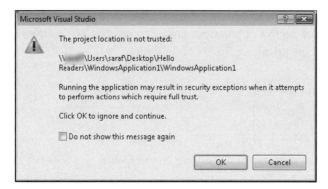

If you want to see this message again, but previously you checked the Do Not Show This Message Again check box, you can go to Tools–Options–Projects And Solutions–General and check the Warn User When The Project Location Is Not Trusted check box.

> ☑ Save new projects when created
> ☑ Warn user when the project location is not trusted
> ☑ Show Output window when build starts

For more information on why UNC shares are not trusted or what to do about it, here's a pointer to the documentation: http://msdn.microsoft.com/en-us/library/bs2bkwxc.aspx.

Build Configurations

The Configuration Manager controls what *flavors* of builds to produce. The simplest of these are Debug, for testing proposes, and Release, for actual end-user use, but you can also create your own. There are various ways of tweaking your build configuration throughout the IDE, but for some projects, a lot of this functionality isn't needed. In these cases, there's a feature called Simplified Build Configurations, which hides a lot of these options.

Tip 7.7: How to use Simplified Build Configurations

> **Sara Aside** The title for this tip as it appears on my blog is "How to pretend the Configuration Manager doesn't exist, besides closing your eyes and saying, 'I don't see you.'" In other words, the Configuration Manager presented an interesting challenge for me as a tester. But Simplified Build Configurations really took it to a new level.

If you have never touched the Debug or Release configurations or have never heard of the Configuration Manager, you might want to try this tip.

Under Tools–Options–Projects And Solutions, you'll see the Show Advanced Build Configurations option. Unchecking this option does quite a few things behind the scenes, but first, I'll briefly describe the Show Advanced Build Configurations option.

> ☑ Track Active Item in Solution Explorer
> ☑ Show advanced build configurations
> ☑ Always show solution

By default, Visual Studio comes with two build configurations: Debug and Release. You are free to create your own build configurations via the Configuration Manager. Check out some of my old blog posts on how the Configuration Manager works, if you want to create your own custom build configurations: *http://blogs.msdn.com/saraford/archive/2005/08/16/452423.aspx* and *http://blogs.msdn.com/saraford/archive/2005/08/18/453346.aspx.*

If you are using a custom build configuration and you uncheck the Show Advanced Build Configuration check box, Visual Studio will pretend you still have it checked, enabling you to still open the Configuration Manager.

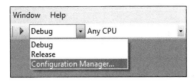

When you are working in Simplified Build Configuration mode, the following happens behind the scenes:

- F5 (*Debug.Start*) runs under the debugger in the Debug configuration. This means that the binaries will be produced in a Debug folder in the output file path.

- Ctrl+F5 (*Debug.StartWithoutDebugging*) runs (with no debugger) in Release configuration. This means the binaries are produced in a Release folder in the output file path.

If you change the Build output path (for example, bin\myRelease) and use *Debug.StartWithoutDebugging* (Ctrl+F5), Visual Studio builds the release in the myRelease folder. But if you press F5, Visual Studio still puts it in the Debug folder.

From a UI perspective, Visual Studio hides all access points to the Configuration Manager when in Simplified Build Configuration. For example, the Configuration (Release or Debug) and Platform (Any CPU, and so forth) options disabled on the standard toolbar.

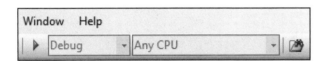

Additionally, the Configuration Manager command disappears on the Solution Explorer context menu, and Configuration and Platform disappear from the Project Properties–Debug page.

And that's more than I ever wanted to type about Simplified Build Configurations, and probably more than you ever wanted to know, but at least now you understand what that little option does. =)

Solution Explorer

The Solution Explorer contains all the files associated with your project (or projects), and obviously, it also contains your solution. Regardless of how much time you spend in the IDE, you are almost guaranteed to use the Solution Explorer at some point, whether it is to add a reference to the project or simply open a file. This section explores some tips on how to customize and navigate the Solution Explorer.

Tip 7.8: How to show the Miscellaneous Files project in the Solution Explorer

On the Tools–Options–Environment–Documents page, you'll find the Show Miscellaneous Files In Solution Explorer option.

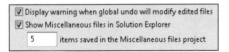

I find this feature very useful when I'm constantly looking at the same files that live outside my current solution. For example, when writing test cases, I would have the actual test case code as its own solution and just reference the test library DLLs. When stepping through the test library, these files get collected under the Miscellaneous Files project. Yes, Miscellaneous Files is actually a project.

When you reopen the solution, the various miscellaneous files will tag along, just how you left them, provided you have the subsequent option *X* Items Saved In The Miscellaneous Files Project set to something greater than 0.

Tip 7.9: There is type-ahead selection support in the Solution Explorer

> **Sara Aside** I've been coming up with little songs to keep sane as I post a daily tip for Visual Studio. I have people swear that they'll catch me on tape singing these one day. One of them is sung to the tune of the Dunkin' Donuts jingle of "Gotta make the donuts" which is "Gotta do tip of the day." Another one I'm trying to perfect is sung to the tune of Phil Collins's "Come Dance into the Light" with "It's the simple things in life!" Sad, but true.

I think this tip is really cool. I didn't know this one until a coworker showed me, and this was after five years of working on the Visual Studio team.

The Solution Explorer supports type-ahead selection, so wherever you are in the tree view, just start typing the full name of your file and the focus will jump to that match, whether a partial match or a full file name match.

Tip 7.10: You can add a solution to a solution

Today's tip falls into the "You can do *what!?*" category.

1. Open your primary solution (the solution you want to add another solution to).

2. Go to File–Add–Add Existing Project.

3. Change Files Of Type to Solution Files.

4. Select the solution file you want to add.

These steps add the contents of ClassLibrary2.sln to the ConsoleApplication1 solution, as shown here.

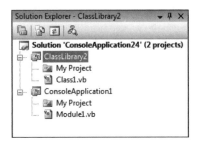

Tip 7.11: You can automatically perform a rename within an entire project when you rename a file in the Solution Explorer

Let's say you create a new class file called Class1. If you try to rename Class1 in the Solution Explorer, Visual Studio prompts you to decide whether you want to rename all references to this code element in your project.

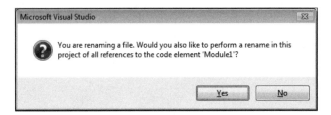

But I'm more of an IDE tips know-it-all, so the real "Did you know" here is this: Did you know you can disable this prompt and just have Visual Studio automatically do the rename for you?

Go to Tools–Options–Projects And Solutions–General and uncheck the Prompt For Symbolic Renaming When Renaming Files option.

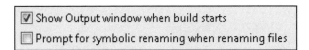

Tip 7.12: How to hide or show a solution in the Solution Explorer

Sometimes, you might find yourself in a state where the solution is not shown. For example, some of the default environment settings, like the Visual Basic Development Settings, have this behavior enabled.

If you find yourself in this state and want the solution back, go to Tools–Options–Projects And Solutions–General and check the Always Show Solution check box.

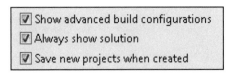

Having said all this, I'll warn you that Visual Studio overrides this setting and always shows the solution if the solution has two or more projects in it.

Tip 7.13: How to have the Solution Explorer always show (or not show) the file currently opened in the editor

Because the default is to have the Track Active Item In Solution Explorer option enabled in the General Development Settings, a more appropriate tip is one that shows you either how to turn it back on or how to turn it off.

On the Tools–Options–Projects And Solutions–General page, there's the Track Active Item In Solution Explorer check box. When enabled, this option will sync your Solution Explorer with the open document.

☑ Always show Error List if build finishes with errors
☑ Track Active Item in Solution Explorer
☑ Show advanced build configurations

Debugging

This section covers IDE-related tips on debugging, including Tools Options settings and tool windows found only while debugging. This section also explores how to debug multiple projects.

Tracepoints

On a given line of code where you want to log the value of a variable, you can use the old-fashioned way of doing a *Console.WriteLine()* or a *PrintF()*. But in Visual Studio 2008, there's a new feature called Tracepoints that allows you to print out these debug statements without modifying your code. Hence, there's no having to go back and delete code prior to a check-in or unwanted debugging info getting released into deployment.

Tip 7.14: You can use tracepoints to log *PrintF()* or *Console.WriteLine()* info without editing your code

Right-click in the editor wherever you want to insert a tracepoint, select Breakpoint, and then select Insert Tracepoint.

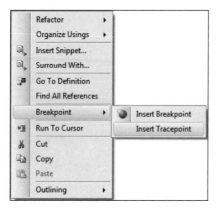

This brings up the tracepoint dialog box, which gives you some helpful default settings. But for this example, the really helpful default is in the descriptive text for logging the contents of a variable.

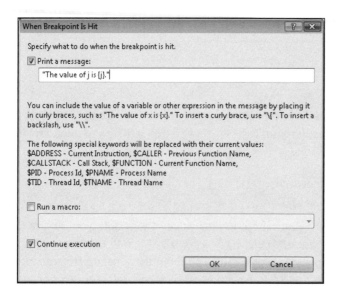

You'll notice that the editor shows a diamond instead of a circle.

```
static void Main(string[] args)
{
    for (int i = 0,j = 0; i < 20; i++)
    {
        j = i++;
    }
}
```

And the tracepoints are logged in the Output window's Debug pane.

```
Output
Show output from: Debug                    ▼ | ⏸ | ⏩ ⏭ | ⏯ | ⏎
"The value of j is 0."
"The value of j is 2."
"The value of j is 4."
"The value of j is 6."
"The value of j is 8."
"The value of j is 10."
"The value of j is 12."
"The value of j is 14."
"The value of j is 16."
◄                    Ⅲ
```

Breakpoints

Where would debugging be without breakpoints? This section covers the basics of break-points, including the various ways to set breakpoints and how to set conditions on them.

Tip 7.15: You can set a breakpoint by clicking the indicator margin

Sara Aside I'm very big into starting off with the basics, just in case someone reading this didn't know about this tip.

You can set a breakpoint on any applicable line by clicking the indicator margin, as illustrated here.

```
class Program
{
    static void Main(string[] args)
    {
        Console.WriteLine("I need a break");
    }         Click here to insert a
}             breakpoint on this line
```

Clicking here inserts the breakpoint, as shown next.

```
class Program
{
    static void Main(string[] args)
    {
        Console.WriteLine("I need a break");
    }
}
```

Tip 7.16: You can press F9 to set a breakpoint on the current line

The command *Debug.ToggleBreakpoint* sets (or deletes) the breakpoint on the current line, in case you don't want to take your hands off the keyboard.

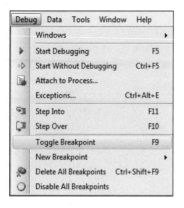

Tip 7.17: You can use Ctrl+F9 to enable or disable a breakpoint

I didn't see this command under the Debug menu. So, in case you want to use the keyboard to enable or disable a breakpoint, you can press Ctrl+F9, which is bound to the command *Debug.EnabledBreakpoint*. Note that you won't find a *Debug.DisableBreakpoint* because this is handled by the enabled command.

```
class Program
{
    static void Main(string[] args)
    {
        Console.WriteLine("I need a break");
    }
}
```

A disabled breakpoint still gets saved in your Breakpoints window, even though it will not get hit during debugging.

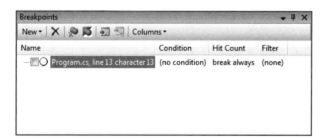

Tip 7.18: You can set conditional breakpoints

When you want to break only under certain conditions, you can right-click a breakpoint red circle (or go to the Breakpoints window and bring up the context menu on a given breakpoint) and select Condition to bring up the dialog box for conditional breakpoints.

You're given two options: break only when the specified expression is true, or break only when the specified value has changed. For this example, because I'm in a *for* loop, I'll break when the value of *i* is greater than 5.

You'll notice that the breakpoint circle now has a red plus on it to indicate it is conditional.

Tip 7.19: You can use breakpoint filters to break the right process

Conditional breakpoints are for breaking at the expression level, when a particular condition is true, like $x = 5$. But what if you have multiple instances of the same app running? How do you set to break the instance you want?

The answer is breakpoint filters.

Go to Tools–Options–Debugging–General, and you'll see the option Enable Breakpoint Filters.

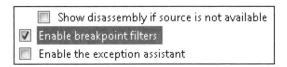

Set a breakpoint and right-click to bring up the context menu.

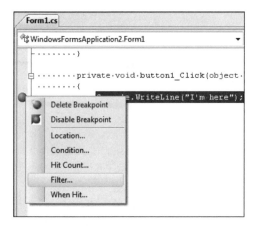

In the Breakpoint Filter dialog box, you can specify when to break. The next image shows breaking a process by its process ID.

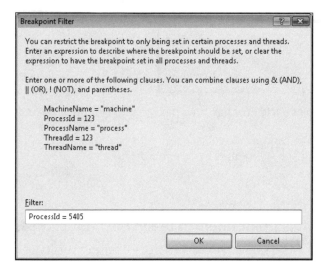

And you can verify the breakpoint filter in the Breakpoints window under the Filter column.

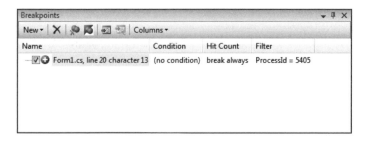

Tip 7.20: You can press Ctrl+B to set a breakpoint at the desired function

In case you want to set a breakpoint at a given function, and not at the current line, you don't have to search for the function name and then hit F9. Instead, you can press Ctrl+B to run the Break At Function command.

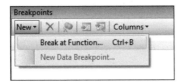

This command brings up the New Breakpoint window.

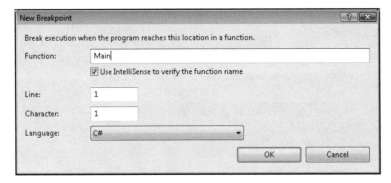

Here you can type the name of the function you want to set a new breakpoint at.

Tip 7.21: You can press Ctrl+Alt+B to open the Breakpoints window

Under Debug–Windows, you'll find the Breakpoints window.

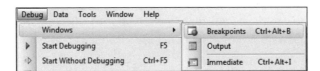

The keyboard shortcut is Ctrl+Alt+B, which is bound to the command *Debug.Breakpoints*.

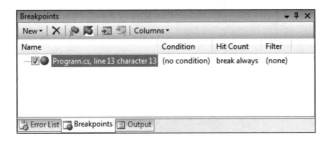

Tip 7.22: You can press Ctrl+Shift+F9 to delete all breakpoints

You can press Ctrl+Shift+F9, bound to *Debug.DeleteAllBreakpoints*, to delete all the break-points you've created in your solution. The command is found under the Debug menu.

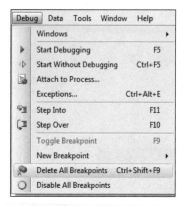

The option is also found on the Breakpoints window in the toolbar.

Tip 7.23: You can disable the warning message before you delete all breakpoints

The previous tip talked about how to delete all breakpoints. If you are following along at home, you have encountered the warning message that appears when you attempt to do this.

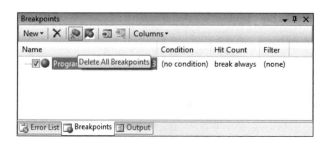

If you find it annoying, you can disable it by going to Tools–Options–Debugging–General and unchecking the Ask Before Deleting All Breakpoints option.

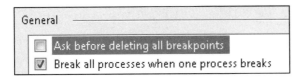

DataTips

DataTips are very similar to the Watch window. (See the Watch window tips that appear later in the chapter.) However, unlike the Watch window, where you have to navigate to a tool window, DataTips allow you to keep your focus in the editor.

Tip 7.24: You can use DataTips to edit a variable's content

Whenever you are debugging and want to change the contents of a variable, you can drag the variable into the Watch window. But you can also use DataTips to change the variable without leaving the editor.

Hover over a variable when you have hit a breakpoint. You'll notice a glorified ToolTip appear. This is actually a DataTip. You can click the value of the variable to go into an edit mode. Change the contents of the variable, and press Enter to commit.

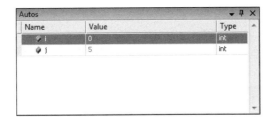

If you have the Autos window open, you'll notice the color change, implying the commit was successful.

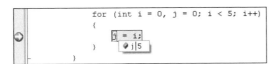

Multiple Projects

If you are using only one project per solution, this section may not have too much significance for you. But if you have multiple projects, you can select which ones you want started under the debugger.

Tip 7.25: How to select the startup project from the Solution Explorer

There are two ways you can select a project as the startup project when you have more than one project in your solution.

The first way is via the Solution Property pages. Right-click the solution node in the Solution Explorer, and under Common Properties–Startup Project, you can choose Single Startup Project. Now you can select which project you want.

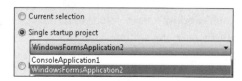

The second way is to right-click the project and select the Set As StartUp Project command from the context menu.

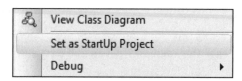

The startup project appears in bold in the Solution Explorer.

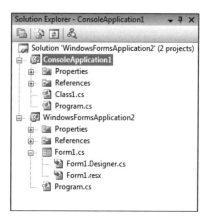

Tip 7.26: You can start debugging multiple projects

> **Sara Aside** This tip marked the one-year anniversary of doing the "Tip of the Day" series. I consider July 27, 2007, as the kick-off date of "Tip of the Day." Wow, what a difference a post a day makes!
>
> Thanks to everyone who has been reading the series. It's been an extremely rewarding experience to see these tips help people. And I also want to express my thanks for all the motivation you have given me to continue writing. It takes me on the average 20 to 30 minutes to decide what tip to write, to capture the screen shots, and to add it to the queue. I refuse to do the math to see just how many puppies I could have potty-trained by now. I just don't want to know. =D

Right-click the solution in the Solution Explorer, and select Properties. Go to the Common Properties–Startup Project page. (It's the first page in the dialog box.)

You'll see three option buttons:

- **Current Selection** This option selects whichever project had the inactive selection (that is, whichever project was selected previously) when you went to the Solution Property Pages.

- **Single Startup Project** Usually this is the first project you had in the solution, or it's the project that you manually set as the startup project.

- **Multiple Startup Projects** And there was great joy! When this option is enabled, you can pick and choose which projects to start (and make sure you choose Start and not Start Without Debugging).

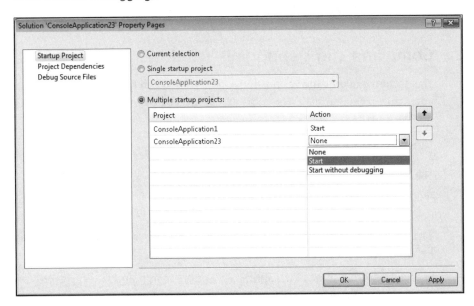

And using the preceding example, when I hit F5, I get the following.

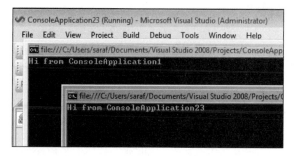

Tip 7.27: How to have all processes break when one process breaks

In Tools–Options–Debugging–General, there's the option Break All Processes When One Process Breaks.

Let's say you are debugging multiple projects, and you want to configure what happens when one process breaks.

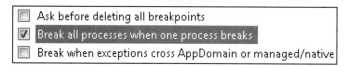

For example, let's say I have two console applications running in an infinite loop. On the second console application, I break the process. If I have checked the Break All Processes When One Process Breaks check box, the first console application will break also.

And, of course, you can uncheck this option to have the first console application keep going.

Compiling and Debugging Windows

This section explores the various tool windows you can use while compiling and debugging your code, including the Error List view, Watch window, and Immediate Window.

Error List

The Error List does exactly as its name suggests. It lists all the errors in your solution, alongside any warnings and messages.

Tip 7.28: You can use Ctrl+Shift+F12 to view the next error listed in the Error List

The keyboard binding is Ctrl+Shift+F12, and the command is *View.NextError*. I'm a little surprised that there isn't a default keyboard shortcut for *View.PreviousError*. But you can always add one yourself.

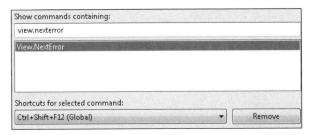

And, of course, the status bar tries to be helpful by showing you the error you have navigated to. =)

Tip 7.29: How to customize your Error List view

Sara Aside   This was one of my least favorite designs in the IDE. When the Error List was split from the Task List in Visual Studio 2005, a row of buttons was put on the top of the Error List for users to customize whether they wanted to see just Errors, Warnings, or Messages. But, then again, it enables me to show you cool tips like Tip 7.32.

For example, here's the default with everything enabled.

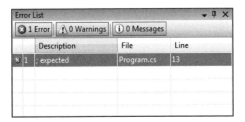

And now, here's the Error List with nothing enabled, for dramatic effect.

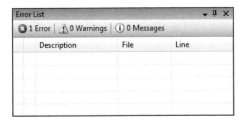

Tip 7.30: You can view an error's documentation directly from the Error List

If you right-click an error in the Error List view, you'll see a context menu pop up with the Show Error Help option.

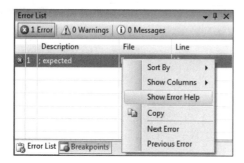

Clicking this command launches the external documentation viewer, also known as dexplorer in some social circles, to that specific error.

Tip 7.31: You can do multicolumn sorting (secondary sort, and so forth) in both the Error List and the Task List

Both the Error List and the Task List have support for multicolumn sorting, such as secondary sort and tertiary sort.

For example, suppose you want to sort all tasks (or errors) by file first and then by line number so that you can go through each file in the order in which the tasks (or errors) appear.

To do a secondary sort, follow these steps:

1. Click the column that you want to have as the primary sort (such as File).

2. Shift+Click on the column you want to have as a secondary sort (such as Line number).

3. Rinse and repeat for other columns.

For the Error List, you can see how things are sorted first by File and then by Line number.

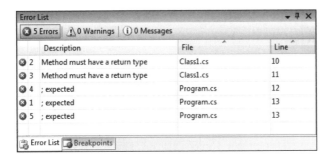

Tip 7.32: You can bind the show Errors, Warnings, and Messages buttons to keyboard shortcuts

> **Sara Aside** In the "Tip of the Day" series on my blog, this tip was entry number 200. Considering how I blogged a new tip about Visual Studio every day, it is amazing to think what a difference a day makes. At the time of this writing, I'm approaching number 300!

I'm excited about this tip. Not because it is tip number 200—this was purely coincidental—but because I accidentally found it while browsing the commands in the Tools–Options–Environment–Keyboard page that contained the word *Error*.

Go to Tools–Options–Environment–Keyboard, and search for *Errors*. You'll notice that this odd Errors command will stare back at you.

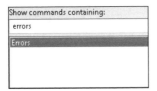

I say this "odd" command because usually Visual Studio commands have the canonical name format of *<word>.<word>*. This obviously caught my eye, so I contacted the developer for confirmation.

These commands toggle the Errors, Warnings, and Messages shown on the Error List, so you can bind them to keyboard shortcuts.

For example, you could bind the following commands to the keyboard shortcuts shown:

- Errors: Ctrl+Alt+Shift+E

- Warnings: Ctrl+Alt+Shift+W

- Messages: Ctrl+Alt+Shift+M

Now, instead of clicking the buttons, you can just use the keyboard shortcut. Pretty cool.

Tip 7.33: How to show or prevent the Error List from appearing after a failed build

Usually the Error List is shown (whether it is autohiding or just closed) whenever a build fails with errors. If you like using just the Output window (because you can double-click an error message in the Output window and jump to that line), here's how to prevent the Error List from appearing.

Under Tools–Options–Projects And Solutions–General, there's the Always Show Error List If Build Finishes With Errors check box. Uncheck this option to prevent the Error List from appearing after a failed build.

☐ Always show Error List if build finishes with errors
☑ Track Active Item in Solution Explorer
☑ Show advanced build configurations

Watch Window

The Watch window (or Watch windows, because you can have up to four of them) not only provides a way for you to keep track of your variables and their contents, it also allows you to make changes to the contents of your variables.

Tip 7.34: You can use the Watch window to quickly change a variable's value

Have you ever been debugging some code and wanted to quickly change a variable's value without having to stop debugging? Here's what to do.

Add the value to the Watch window. You can select the variable and drag it into the Watch window as shown here.

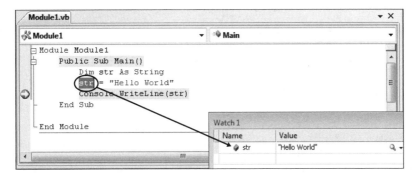

Then double-click the variable's contents within the Watch window, and you'll be able to edit.

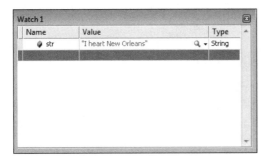

Either click outside this field or press Enter to commit the change, and the variable will contain the new contents.

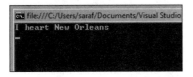

If you need to clear the Watch window's variable contents, just hit Delete on that row.

Tip 7.35: You can view numeric values in hexadecimal format in your debug windows

The debug tool windows (Locals, Autos, and Watch window) have a context menu that includes the Hexadecimal Display command. Just in case you ever needed to see values in hexadecimal, you now know how to do it.

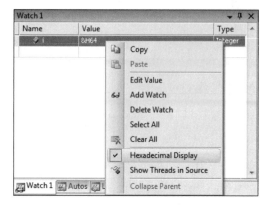

Immediate Window

When you want to do more than just edit the value of a variable, you can rewrite entire functions or create new ones in the Immediate Window.

Tip 7.36: You can use the Immediate Window as a glorified calculator or side-debugger within your debugger

Sara Aside I found the Immediate Window especially useful when I was doing the math to automate dragging a tool window from a docked location to a docking target. I basically had to do the math to calculate a straight line between the two points in order to send the coordinates to the mouse drag functions. If I did the math incorrectly (and the inside joke here is I have a math degree), I could pull up the Immediate Window and play with the calculations over and over again without interfering with the main debugger. This means that the variables and state of the main debugger would remain the same, unless I purposefully modified a value in the Immediate Window.

Let's start off with a very simple example. Let's say that you have the basic "Hello World" console app, but you want to print out the result of some calculation. Notice how the console app just has "Hello World."

If I put a breakpoint at the very end of this simple console app, I can bring up the Immediate Window via Debug–Windows–Immediate and do whatever I need. Let's say I needed to use the Immediate Window as a glorified calculator. I can figure out the value of 1 + 1, as shown in this Visual Basic console app.

```
Immediate Window
i = 1+1
?i
2 {Integer}
```

Since we're in a console application, we can even have the value of *i* printed to the console window via the Immediate Window.

```
Immediate Window
i = 1+1
?i
2 {Integer}
Console.WriteLine(i.ToString())
```

And now the value of *2* appears in the console window.

```
file:///C:/Users/saraf/Documents/Visual
Hello World
2
```

Appendix A
Visual Studio Factoids

While I was preparing a talk titled "Microsoft Visual Studio 2008 IDE Tips and Tricks" at the Microsoft TechEd Developers Conference 2008, Rob Caron, a marketing manager for Visual Studio, suggested I put together a list of Visual Studio factoids consisting of little-known facts about the history of Visual Studio. The first person who came to my mind to interview was Douglas Hodges, a principal architect on the Visual Studio team. Many of us believe he knows everything about the inner workings of the IDE architecture. Doug has been with the team since the Visual C++ 5.0 days and has seen many, many things.

I had asked my blog readers for their questions regarding Visual Studio's history or its implementation to see what questions were missing from my own personal wish list. I'm really glad I didn't try to put together the list by myself as a surprise to the readers, because they had a better list of questions than I could have ever thought of.

While I was interviewing Doug, he called Pat Brenner for help. Pat is not only a long time Visual Studio developer but a developer at Microsoft for well over 20 years. It was a really cool experience to interview these two long-time Visual Studio team members.

Both Doug and Pat suggested I contact Donna Wallace Zuest, another 20+ year Microsoft employee and a senior user-experience designer for Visual Studio, for more background information regarding design and style decisions.

Visual Studio Q&A

The following sections are my notes from my conversation with Doug Hodges, Pat Brenner, and Donna Wallace Zuest.

Why is the executable file called devenv.exe instead of visualstudio.exe?

The original concept for the Visual Studio IDE was that the IDE would be a brand less, empty, extensible shell that hosted multiple products simultaneously. When the shell was empty, the title bar would display the generic name "Microsoft Development Environment." However, when the user was focused on editing assets that belonged to a project, the title bar would change to show the name of that product (for example, "Microsoft Visual Basic .NET," "Microsoft Visual C# .NET," or "*<name of VSIP product>*." Not only would the title bar name change but the *Help.About* command name would change to reflect the currently active product (for example, Help.About Microsoft Visual Basic .NET).

The Visual Studio IDE has a strong notion of tracking context and displaying only the appropriate commands for the current context. Thus, when the IDE is focused on a form or class file from a Visual Basic project, all the commands of the product are tailored to be appropriate for a Visual Basic project. The commands for the C++ project disappear. The changing title bar was part of the feedback the IDE provided to help the user understand what context is active. The name of the empty IDE was "Microsoft Development Environment" because the application was focused on being a great tool for developer activities. The application's executable file became a derivative of the generic IDE name "Microsoft Development Environment" or "Development Environment," or "devenv" for short.

The concept for the generic environment even precedes the Visual Studio IDE time frame. The Visual C++ IDE was named msdev.exe for a similar reason as devenv.exe. It was conceived as a general IDE platform that could host multiple plug-in products, based on Microsoft Foundation Class (MFC) extension dynamic-link libraries (DLLs). Visual InterDev also shipped using this generic environment.

The next-generation IDE shell, known today as the Visual Studio IDE or devenv.exe, was based on a COM plug-in architecture, which enables independently versioning components to communicate with one another. This new IDE was created by using the Visual Basic shell and stripping out all the product-specific functionality. Then Visual Basic .NET had to be re-created in this new IDE as a package, even though it was their original IDE to begin with.

Starting in Visual Studio 2005, a stronger branding identity was given to the Visual Studio product. The title bar was updated to display "Microsoft Visual Studio" all the time. The *Help. About* command was changed to the static text Help.About Microsoft Visual Studio. Despite these branding changes, the executable's file name remained the same.

Is the Visual Studio logo an infinity symbol or Möbius strip?

It is an infinity symbol. I had great hopes it would turn out to be a Möbius strip.

What do the colors in the Visual Studio logo signify?

The colors in the logo are the Microsoft corporate colors.

Solution Explorer: Is it on the left side or right side of the IDE?

This was one of the big debates of the day.

In Microsoft Visual Basic, the Solution Explorer was on the right side of the IDE. In Microsoft Visual C++, it appeared on the left side. Both groups of developers were very used to their layouts after so many versions and wanted to retain their legacy layouts.

While the Visual Studio team was merging all the shells into the one IDE during the Visual Studio .NET 2002 product cycle, the decision was made to have the Solution Explorer appear on the right side of the IDE. I started my career at Microsoft toward the end of the Visual Studio .NET 2002 product cycle, so I wasn't able to witness any of these debates firsthand.

Why is there a "Solution" concept?

This was *the big debate*.

Visual Basic had project groups, and Visual C++ had .dsw files or workspaces. In Visual C++, a workspace always existed, even if it consisted of just one project. Additionally, you could also open any random file in Visual C++, unlike in Visual Basic.

The big debate when the single IDE was being formed was which behavior to use. It was agreed to go with the Visual C++ approach on the condition that a new name would be used to describe this concept. And hence, a "Solution" was created.

A little-known fact that surprised me while chatting with Pat is that we actually put support into the UI for using a string other than the word "Solution," such as Workspace or Master Project. It was originally inserted for testing purposes, and we shipped the product with it at least once. I've been unable to figure out which version included that or to create a screen shot of the UI, as it has since been removed.

Why Are the Tool Window Tabs Shown at the Bottom of a Tool Window Group and the File Tabs Are at the Top of the File Tab Channel?

Recall in Chapter 4, "Manage your Environment layout" how you can put a tool window into a tabbed document state, so that it appears among the open files in the file tab channel. But, you can't move or dock an open file outside the file tab channel like you can with a tool window.

When the notion of tabbed documents was introduced in Visual Studio 6, it was intended to be a way to easily manage many open files. The original design actually provided a way for tool windows and document windows to dock to each other in a free-form way. In other words, you could dock tool windows to specific documents and create all kinds of configurations.

The problem with this design was that tool windows are not multi-instance, meaning you cannot have the same tool window open multiple times. Users would close documents and lose any docked tool windows. It was difficult to find these tool windows again to reopen them.

The user-experience designers created a rule that only files and tool windows in the tabbed document state could appear in the file tab channel. Tool windows could dock anywhere as long as they were in the dockable state, but files could not be docked. To help reinforce the difference, tool window tabs are displayed at the bottom of a tool window group, and file tabs are displayed at the top of the file tab channel.

Why is Common7 not Common8 or Common9?

This is a known issue. Only the root folder should contain a version number.

Appendix B
Tips on Blogging Tips

When I agreed to write a "Tip of the Day" series on my blog, I didn't quite realize what I was getting myself into. I had learned a lot from the weekly series I had written in the Visual Studio 2005 days, so I was somewhat prepared. Rob Caron, a marketing manager for Visual Studio, and I put together a formula for the daily series, something I didn't have for the weekly series. But still, nothing can prepare you for what life has in store when you agree to a daily blog post. Fortunately for me, "Tip of the Day" doesn't work on weekends.

Nothing can quite prepare you for the realization that when you do a "Tip of the Day" blog, you really have to write a new tip *every single day*. This includes the days when you get really busy at work, the days when you go on vacation, and especially the days when you get sick or injured. You have to be prepared for the unexpected.

I'm obviously a big fan of community, and I love sharing what I've learned during my seven years at Microsoft. Therefore, I would be remiss not to share tips on how to do a "Tip of the Day" series, in case you decide to do something similar. And let me know if you go for it, so I can cheer you on, just like my blog readers did with their "Go Sara Go" comments at *http://blogs.msdn.com/saraford/archive/2008/03/18/did-you-know-sara-turns-30-today-so-i-need-another-go-sara-go-and-how-to-use-safemode-174.aspx.*

Secret "Tip Of The Day" Formula

In May 2007, Rob Caron and I brainstormed about what this formula would look like. He introduced me to the book *Made to Stick: Why Some Ideas Survive and Others Die* by Chip and Dan Heath (Random House, 2007). We applied some of the principles from the book to make the tips more memorable.

Tip 1: Focus on one specific action per tip

The idea is to keep the tips as simple as possible. Instead of focusing on end-to-end functionality, the tips focus on how to do one specific thing. For example, the settings located in Tools Options fall perfectly into this category. I consider each tip to be an explanation of how each option works. My reasoning is to provide readers with information on how the individual pieces work, so they are able to mix and match these pieces to best suit their needs.

Tip 2: Provide an image with each tip

It is amazing how a picture brings a blog entry to life. Now imagine what it does for a tip. It was a requirement (yes, I require myself to do things) that each tip have a picture, regardless of what the tip was about. Sometimes I needed several pictures to illustrate the tip, and sometimes it was a real challenge to come up with a single image. Even a tip about a keyboard shortcut required an image. Even if I had to draw a tree, which amused me greatly, every tip has an image.

Tip 3: Reference a credible source

Many times I had to ask the feature developer, "Hey, what does this do, again?" or "Um, I think I broke it, but I'm not sure." Whenever I had to ask for help, I always mentioned it in the blog entry. I think sharing common struggles goes a long way in building a community of readers.

Tip 4: Share and collect stories whenever possible

Many times, I felt compelled to share a story about the tip. Initially, I had wanted to include one story per tip, but I quickly realized that I shouldn't try to force stories if a tip just didn't have one.

Then, at one point in the latter half of the "Tip of the Day" series, the idea came to me that I could ask blog readers for their opinions about the tips, how they used the tip, or how they didn't use the tip. I realized that the tips were not only providing the "how to" information but also starting a "Let's discuss this feature today" thread. After this light-bulb moment, my concerns about providing stories definitely decreased, but I still have to write a tip every day.

Tip 5: Queue up your tips far, far in advance

This should be a given, based on what I said earlier about vacations, illness, workload, and all the other things that happen in life when you make plans. The further out you can queue your tips, the happier you will be in your "Tip of the Day" life. Also, I highly recommend using a wall calendar so that you can keep track of where you are in your queue and plan for the expected interruptions, such as holidays, vacations, and birthdays.

Tip 6: Set your tips to go live before dawn

Another thing that caught me off guard was time zones. I live in Washington State, and I didn't consider that a tip that goes live at 9 a.m. Pacific standard time (PST) won't arrive in people's RSS readers until after noon on the East Coast. It's not really a tip of the day for them, but more like a tip in the afternoon.

I realized this issue the hard way about the second week into the series, when Rob Caron shot me an e-mail saying, "What happened to today's tip?" I was just starting to queue tips in advance and accidentally had one ready to go live in the afternoon, instead of morning. The East Coast people probably thought the series was already over in just a week's time.

Nonetheless, I corrected the error and decided tips should go out at 3 a.m. PST. Publishing at this time addressed two concerns:

1. The East Coast people would get a tip in their RSS reader first thing in the morning.

2. If I ever made this mistake again, I could correct it first thing in the morning PST time, still giving everyone in the United States their "Tip of the Day."

At the time of this writing, all tips have gone out at 3 a.m. on the first try.

Tip 7: Use Windows Live Writer to write and queue your tips

Shameless Microsoft plug? No! I tell it like it is, and I bow to this great and wonderful tool. Seriously, I can't image doing "Tip of the Day" without it. I can queue my tips into the future. The calendar control helps me to not tip on weekends. And I can save drafts if I'm waiting for clarification on a tip. I can even see how my blog entry will appear according to my blog's CSS while not connected to the Internet.

By far, the best thing about Live Writer is how well it works in offline mode. I have written many tips while on airplanes and other places where I didn't have Internet connectivity. And when I return home, I can simply publish the tips and celebrate much happiness in "Tip of the Day" land, knowing the series lives on.

But check out Live Writer and see for yourself at *http://get.live.com/writer/overview*.

Appendix C
Software Testing Tips

During my four-and-a-half years as a software design engineer in test on the Visual Studio team, I picked up a great many things beyond just the ins and outs of Visual Studio. When I first started blogging about software testing, I was pleasantly surprised at how many people found it interesting. They let me know by linking to my blog, leaving comments on my blog posts, and sending their interview questions for me to answer. Well, they sent me their questions, but I didn't answer them. =D

Five Tips for Surviving as a Tester

Following are some of the lessons I learned from testing the Visual Studio IDE. Whether you are a professional tester or you just do software testing occasionally, you may find these tips to be helpful.

Tip 1: Never assume anything

I frequently tell two stories about how I learned this tip the hard way.

Story number one begins during my first six months at Microsoft, during which time I was assigned my first project where I was the only tester. We had just deployed a Web site internally within the Microsoft corporate network as an alpha release to collect internal feedback. Not even 20 minutes went by before the developer sent an e-mail message saying that the site was throwing errors in the most common scenarios. That was the first time I experienced that tester "state of shock," where you thought you had tested it all but something obvious apparently slipped by you.

Based on the call stack, it didn't take the developer long to figure out that one of the check-box labels was causing the error. This check box was the only one of all the check boxes that contained a forward slash (/) or any special character. Both the program manager and the developer looked at me and said, "Did you test this?" Let's just say those are words that no tester *ever* wants to hear. I took a deep breath and admitted the truth, which was that I had assumed that since the first row of check boxes worked, the rest of them would work too. In other words, I had no idea whether it had been a last-minute regression or whether the bug had existed all along.

The program manager picked up the phone and called the server administrator, asking if he would do a favor for us and start the server. If I recall correctly, the developer had an idea for a quick fix that would require "only" a start rather than a full deployment. The server started, the site came back up, and the mainline scenario was still broken. The developer then thought of another idea, but the program manager said that he couldn't ask for another favor.

The lesson I learned from story number one is to never assume that any basic functionality will just work. Story number two occurred during the latter half of my software testing career, while I was on the editor team. We were in the midst of a full test pass for the Visual Studio 2005 Beta 2 release, where every known test case must be run and every possible scenario must be tried in order to break the software. I recall some feature areas having so many test cases that it took three weeks to run them all, and most of them were automated!

A full test pass is usually a tester's last chance to have bugs of medium and even low priority fixed before the release, but it is specifically designed to find the high-priority bugs first. Because many of these tests are automated, we had a lot of analysis to do in the lab, such as figuring out why the test case failed. Was it a product bug? Was it a test-case logic issue? Was it just a UI-timing issue, where the UI experiences a delay in showing a window but the automation framework attempts to run the command a little too soon, hence failing the test? While analyzing test-case failures for some of the primary scenarios, I couldn't help think about how many test cases I had to run and analyze. In other words, I wanted to analyze failures as fast as possible.

I will never forget this one in the lab *run*, a term we use to describe running specific test cases against a specific machine configuration or edition of Visual Studio. This run was testing the Visual Studio Standard edition. All the Emacs and Brief emulation test cases, which verify alternate editing functionality and keyboard shortcuts, failed.

A quick investigation showed that the required files were not found on the computer that the run was conducted on. I assumed that the missing files obviously had something to do with the run itself and not with the actual product. I based this assumption on the fact that the Professional edition, among others, had passed. Also, it wasn't uncommon to see an issue arise with a run configuration, although these issues are more closely investigated than what I was doing.

I analyzed the failures resulting from a machine configuration—that is, failures that happened because the files were not present on the machine. And my analysis came back to haunt me.

Several weeks later, as we were about to ship the beta release, the lead developer for the editor discovered that the editor emulation feature was not available on the Standard edition for the Visual Studio 2005 Beta 2 release. Once again, I experienced that "tester shock," and I felt it probably just as bad as I had in the previous story, as in "Wow, I can't believe I let this one get by me!" I realized that the only words worse to a tester's ears than "Did you test this?" are "Why did you assume this was *not* a bug?"

The lesson I learned from story number two is, When in doubt, get a second opinion whether something is a bug.

Here are a few other tips related to never assuming anything:

- Never assume that someone else is covering a particular scenario. Test everything that comes to mind, and then test some more. A little overlap never hurts.

- Never assume the people reading your bug will "just get" the bug. Always be as explicit as possible with your steps for reproducing the issue, even when the steps are completely obvious to you. This holds true especially when you attach a picture to your bug. A picture speaks a thousand words, so make sure that the person reading your bug report hears the right 20 to 30 words.

- Never assume that a simple scenario could not be broken. Always, always, always test, even if it is the most trivial example for the most trivial feature you've ever seen. Don't take the chance of having to hear the words, "Did you test this?"

Tip 2: Learn from the bugs you missed

As I became more confident in my software testing skills, I started actively monitoring the bugs filed against my feature area by other people. I became intrigued by pursuing the idea of "What else am I missing?" There were so many days where I stared at my monitor just wondering what I hadn't tried yet. Looking at these other bug reports helped me identify where I had holes in my software testing style, what strategies for breaking software I had yet to learn, what categories of bugs I hadn't seen yet, and so forth. I believe a lot of software testing skill comes from pure experience.

Ask yourself why someone filed a bug report in your feature area that was later fixed. What could you learn from this bug? Are you missing other similar tests? This process could be considered a root-case analysis. But instead of looking at it from a developer's point of view, asking why this bug was introduced, do it from the tester's point of view, asking what you didn't do to catch the bug. You may find it to be a rewarding exercise to try at least once.

Tip 3: Help your developer however possible

I joke a lot about my "You broke it, and I'm telling" attitude about software testing, but in all seriousness, I do not want my developer to feel this way at all. I think communication is the key to producing high-quality software. And I think the more you can do as a software tester to help out your developer, the better you'll communicate and the happier your customers will be with your product.

First, establish trust with your developer. If you say you're going to test something by a given time, get it done. And if the developer needs something, help him or her out as soon as possible. Also, actively seek feedback from your developer on what features are lacking testing, how you can do more testing, and so forth. As is the case for Tip 2, you'll be surprised how many new scenarios you'll come up with just by asking your developer for ideas.

It won't take long to see the benefits of going the distance to help your developer.

Tip 4: Leave appropriate comments when closing bugs

One year, six months, or even just three months (or, for me, three days) from now, you won't remember how you verified that bug fix. If the original steps for reproducing the bug are no longer the same, make sure you leave a comment explaining exactly what you did to verify the fix. Sometimes bugs morph into other bugs, thus the outcome of the bug doesn't match the original description or even the title!

And don't forget to include the build number when you verify the fix. This will help greatly to identify when regressions are introduced.

Tip 5: Don't just get it in writing

E-mail messages aren't enough. If you're not going to cover a specific scenario, get it in writing in your test plan. Make sure any discussions about bugs, whether they are hallway conversations or conversations via e-mail, are also captured in the bug itself. Unlike e-mail messages that can be quickly discarded and deleted, bug histories tend to stick around much longer. This is especially important if you leave the project, as the person taking over may not know about these conversations or decisions.

Appendix D
How I Started Programming

My story with computers begins when my parents got me a Texas Instruments TI-99 4A Personal Home Computer when I was five years old. To run software on the TI, you purchased cartridges that you would slide into the computer, right alongside the built-in keyboard. Later, I got a cassette deck for saving code and a speech synthesizer, but the games that took advantage of speech were boring. The color monitor was a standalone monitor.

I can remember toying with the TI for many years, probably until I was 12 or 13. Strategy games such as flight simulators greatly captured my attention throughout my childhood.

Hunt the Wumpus

One of the earliest TI computer games I can remember playing is "Hunt the Wumpus." It's a simple strategy game, sometimes studied in artificial intelligence classes, where you have to navigate out of a maze without falling into a pit or running into the wumpus. The TI version scared me to tears every time I ran into the wumpus. The screen would completely change to red, displaying an angry wumpus with the classic "you lost"-style music playing in the background. To a five year old, this was quite traumatic, but somehow I would find the courage to crawl out from under the bed and play the game again. I was just way too fascinated with the computer to let that wumpus get the best of me.

I recall having an equal collection of educational software and video games for the TI. I especially remember the math educational games. I learned how to multiply in second grade by playing the math game—in my elementary school at the time, multiplication and division weren't taught until the third grade. I also remember being scolded by my second-grade teacher for inappropriately correcting her or something along those lines. Hey, she was the one who said that you couldn't subtract a bigger number from a smaller number, like 7 minus 20. I remember being really excited when I screamed, "Yes you can! It is a negative 13!" That was the only bad memory I have of that teacher, so I think I just got her on a bad day. Or more likely, I was just overly excited, which I still get accused of from time to time even today. I was the kind of kid who would have the customer service desk at the local K-Mart page my parents saying that I was lost, just because I wanted to hear my name over the speakers.

Say "YoHo"

Somewhere around that time, when I was in either second or third grade, my parents got me the game "Return to Pirate's Island," written by Scott Adams. This game is the reason I got addicted to playing on a computer. According to his Web site, located at *http://www.msadams.com*, he is the first person to put an "interactive fiction" adventure-style game on a personal computer. He did this in 1978, which coincidentally is the year I was born.

"Return to Pirate's Island" is a text-based game that could also be considered a very light-weight role-playing game, where you play the game from the first-person point of view in the character's shoes. I absolutely *loved* the interaction with the computer. I was just head-over-heels fascinated by the fact that I could type a word into the computer and watch the story line change based upon what I typed. I was determined to figure out one day how the computer knew what to do, how it worked, how it could read English, and so forth.

There was one slight problem with me playing the game. I wasn't quite old enough to read completely on my own. I needed an adult to read at least one word per sentence in the game. So the adult would read the text—something like, "You are in a kitchen. Obvious items are matches and broken glass." And I would instruct the adult to instruct the computer to open the refrigerator. Of course, the adult would have to say, "There is no refrigerator in the kitchen." But I would be quick to point out the contrary to the adult, saying "Of course there's a refrigerator in a kitchen." Annoyed, the adult would type, "open refrigerator," to which the computer would reply, "I don't know what a refrigerator is." I was just absolutely fascinated that in the computer's world a kitchen didn't have a refrigerator. I was determined to figure out why. And for the poor adult (I use a generic description here, because people would alternate translating for me quite frequently), this game went on and on, night after night after night. Even at an early age, I was obsessed with problem solving.

The significance of this story is that it introduced me very early on to the ideas of deterministic algorithms and finite state machines, fundamental concepts for how computers work. To me, it wasn't about winning the game, but rather a challenge to figure out the rules of the computer's world, like why a kitchen didn't have a refrigerator or why I had to wear Scott Adam's "safety sneakers" when I was perfectly safe walking around barefoot in my front yard.

But don't get me wrong, I'm not trying to say I understood college-level computer concepts back then. I also clearly remember reading the introduction and asking my mom what an "armchair pirate" was. Obviously, the author wrote it in the context of stealing software, but as a second-grader, I was quite perplexed why it was a requirement to know how to sail a boat and rob people in order to write a computer game.

It wasn't until my junior year in college that I finally decided I would beat this game once and for all. Thanks to the Internet, I was able to download a version of "Return to Pirate's Island,"

and after nearly 15 years, I finally got past those crocodiles, built the sailboat, and found the treasure.

"Say YoHo, everything spins around, and suddenly, I'm elsewhere ..."

Scott Adams

Thanks, Scott Adams, for the game and for the safety sneakers!

Typing on the TI-99 4A

Around the third or fourth grade, someone in my family got me a book on video game programming for the TI-99 4A. This book probably made the most significant contribution to my interests in computer science. It contained the source code for the video games, but it required you to manually type it in, as there wasn't a concept of "installing" software on the TI. Either the software came on a cartridge or you had to type it in manually. I would two-finger type line after line of code for hours on end. I have to thank my older cousins for taking turns helping me type code on those evenings.

There was this one video game's code in particular that took us many, many hours to type in. The video game involved flying, where you're navigating a fighter-style spaceship through explosive mines and other things that are bad for a spaceship to fly into in space. You could fly at a constant speed in only one direction. All you could do was arrow up or arrow down to avoid destruction. It so ruled.

Just thinking back on those days makes me look at Visual Studio in a much different light. We used a cassette tape deck to store the video games, until it caught on fire one night. Also, we didn't know whether we typed in a letter wrong until the very end of the our typing ordeal, when we got to finally compile. Think of typing on the TI as using Notepad to type hours upon hours of source code from a book, without the ability to save, until the end. Maybe this is why I "heart" Visual Studio so much.

One of the lessons we learned the hard way was that you lost everything if you turned off the computer or if there was a power failure (which of course happened one night). How we were able to ever program that game is beyond me, and we did it on several occasions (as we didn't realize we had to save to cassette the first time). I definitely learned patience, although the adults probably beg to differ, and how to pay attention to detail from all that typing.

Playing Nintendo

Around seventh grade, my mom brought home an IBM computer that took five minutes to start. It originally had MS-DOS 3.0 installed, but over the years I upgraded. There was some castle adventure game for MS-DOS 4.0 that once again captured my full attention, just like "Return To Pirate's Island" did. Only this time, I could actually move my aviator around in the room I was in, instead of the game being text-based only. I don't believe I ever beat that game—probably something else for me to find on the Internet on the next snow day we have in Seattle.

I'll never forget using my first mouse with this computer. I thought the mouse was the coolest thing ever. I also thought printing was cool, but the idea of a paper jam really concerned me, as I thought a paper jam could physically break the printer. Maybe it could have. It was around the time of getting the mouse and printer that I recall learning to study by typing my notes into the computer. Something about the act of typing helped me pay attention to my notes. And there was the added advantage of saving it to a disk, something I cherished from those TI programming days.

Around the same time, I got into Nintendo, just like every other kid on the block. When I beat my first game—"Metroid," a first-person adventure game—I frantically called up all my friends to let them know about the ending. I didn't care that I had beat the game or that Samus, the main character in the game, was a woman. I simply had to share that "They rolled the closing credits, just like in a movie." My friends already knew that I was easily amused, so they weren't surprised by my excitement over seeing the list of names of all the developers who had worked on the game.

The game that really sold me on computer programming—as in, "I want to create video games when I grow up, and no one is getting in my way"—was "Final Fantasy II," a role-playing game for Nintendo. "Final Fantasy II" was the first role-playing game (RPG) that exposed me to not only a story line but character development in a video game. It amazed me to watch these characters think out loud, debate their moral issues, and in some cases even die in the game, not to be brought back to the story line. In a sense, it was an interactive book, where the story line was written but you controlled the pace at which you read the story.

It was also my first RPG that introduced me to side quests, these little extra adventures you could go on that didn't affect the overall outcome of the game. And thanks to the instruction booklet that came with it, I was determined to max out the strength and defenses of my characters, and to find that pink item to get the ultimate weapon.

I was so into this game that I logged nearly 99 hours on it. I wanted to see what would happen to the UI if I played for over 99 hours. Would it give me a special item? Would the UI just freeze at 99 hours? Unfortunately, a cousin wanted to play the game, and I wasn't supervising when he decided which folder to save his newly created game in. Something inside my head snapped when I saw my beloved status showing less than an hour. I've never been able to quite get into RPGs again, although in my adult years, I was able to enjoy "Final Fantasy VII." But that enjoyment was probably because I was recovering from a motorcycle accident and I couldn't do anything but play video games and watch TV.

Shortly after I beat "Final Fantasy II," around the seventieth hour mark, I got a smooth collie from the pound. I named him Cecil, after the main character in the game. He was the most loyal dog in the world to this only child, living up to his namesake in the game. He lived a very long life, 10+ years. Imagine a story line to a video game so intriguing to a kid that the creators got free advertisement for the game for 10 years, all in the name of a dog. I still to this day hear, "You named a dog *Cecil*?" I probably shouldn't tell people that I'm debating calling my next smooth collie "Cecil 2."

Will Solve Math Problems to Code

I went to a very small all-girls Catholic high school in Mississippi that had only 250 students in the entire school. My sophomore year, I really wanted to take this "Intro to Pascal Programming" course, the only course on computer programming offered at the school at the time. But it conflicted with Algebra 2. On a whim, I decided to devote a weekend to doing nothing but answering every question in every chapter of the algebra book. Hey, at least I find constructive ways to deal with my frustrations. But yes, I have way too much energy.

The one weekend turned into roughly five weekends, but I was determined to take that programming class before it was too late to catch up. Finally, the day came when I proudly walked into the Algebra 2 classroom, handed the unsuspecting teacher the notebook, and said, "I'm finished. I can either take the programming course or stay here and be bored for the rest of the year. It's your call."

I got an "A" in the programming course that year.

Studying in College

Needless to say, once I got into college at Mississippi State, it was significantly easier for me to study computer science. My undergraduate advisor, Dr. Donna Reese, was the best, most excellent advisor anyone could ask for. Or to put it into a better perspective, she was able to tame me. Not many people are able to direct my energy effectively, and even fewer are able to get through to me when I'm in one of my "I will drive myself off the cliff" obsessive problem-solving states of mind. Any previous or current manager of mine reading this right now is either cracking up laughing or rolling their eyes in agreement. She inspired me to step up and take a leadership role during my junior year as president of the MSU Student Chapter of the Association of Computing Machinery (ACM), an organization for computer professionals. This leadership role was simply the hands-down best opportunity of my undergraduate career. I consider Dr. Reese to be my first mentor, even though I didn't realize it at the time.

You could say ACM is where I first got a taste of *technical evangelism*, the concept of connecting technology and people. I cannot say how much I thrive on this concept, but then again, some of you already know this because of my "Embrace Open Source on CodePlex" artwork on my Microsoft office window. I loved organizing the freshman class exam study halls, explaining how you can have a tic-tac-toe machine built out of K'NEX, and picking up the foot-long Subway sandwich for the yearly picnic. And there were the practical jokes, like the day I discovered my key to the ACM bulletin board also opened the other bulletin board where all the faculty and staff had their pictures and titles listed.

Oh, and thanks, Dr. Reese, for still answering your cell phone when I call to tell you about the things that amuse me at work. Yes, despite the invention of caller ID, she still answers. =D

Enter Microsoft

During my senior year at Mississippi State, I worked as a research assistant under Dr. John T. Foley on WebTOP, located at *http://www.webtop.org*. I used Microsoft Visual J++ every day for a year to use Virtual Reality Modeling Language (VRML) to simulate physics lab experiments. For example, I wrote the "Laser" module, which simulates a laser beam projecting on a surface, and the "Reflection and Refraction" module, which I explain later.

While writing the "Reflection and Refraction" module, I discovered a bug in Visual J++ where the yellow-highlighted current statement line would get off by one line every time I jumped out of a file. Since my project had numerous files, the current statement would move farther away from the real line being executed the more I tried to debug my program. I would have to keep track of where I was, with pen and paper. It was an incredibly frustrating experience, to say the least.

On the morning of my Microsoft interview, when I found out that I would be interviewing with the Visual Studio team as a Software design engineer in Testing, I was elated. Not just because I would have the opportunity to meet actual members of the team—I was *really* elated because I would be able to tell them about this bug.

Interviewing at Microsoft

In the Building 19 lobby on the Microsoft Redmond Campus, one of the candidates sitting at the table decided she was going to break the silence by having each of us go around and talk about ourselves and the school we went to. As the introductions went around, the names of the schools I heard were MIT, Notre Dame, UCLA, and so forth. I was really nervous hearing the names of these schools, as I had never met anyone who had ever attended these schools before. But I was determined to keep my game face and my focus.

My Software Design Engineer in Testing (SDET) interview started with the Microsoft Exchange team that morning. I had no prior software testing experience, beyond writing the occasional test plan as required in some of my college courses. But I caught on quickly to how they wanted a software tester to approach a problem. I felt pretty overwhelmed with the coding questions, mostly because I was nervous. I don't think I did very well there. I think

I was still feeling so over my head from being in Seattle, at Microsoft, and meeting the other candidates that morning. Fortunately, I had a really good lunch interviewer who allowed me to eat (Thank you! Thank you! Thank you!), so I was in really good shape physically when it was time to interview with the Visual Studio team that afternoon.

I think I did a really good job with the first Visual Studio interviewer. He asked me about WebTOP, and I explained to him how I had written the "Reflection and Refraction" module. It is an animated module that demonstrates in VRML how light can be reflected and refracted between two mediums, like air and water, based on physics equations such as Snell's law. My real-world example was swimming in a pool. If you're at a certain depth, you can still see people standing alongside the pool, but the deeper you get, the less you can see of the surface. While I was explaining how I coded the module, the interviewer said, "Yep, that's Snell's law." I looked at him shocked, with an expression of "How did you know that?" He said, "I was a physics major." I said, "Oh man, I can't believe I just forced you to listen to all of that." He said, "Well, you got it right," in a casual, "it's all good" sort of way.

I don't think I did so well in the second interview on the Visual Studio team. I got caught up analyzing a math problem because I was taking an advanced calculus course at the time, where it's all proofs and no numbers. I tried to write the mathematical proof that a number n cannot be divisible by any number greater than n divided by 2, but I wasn't that good at writing proofs. As soon as I started writing, "For every epsilon in the set of R, there exists...," I knew the interview was over. Advanced Calculus really messed with my head that semester. I think the interviewer was surprised for a couple of reasons:

1. I attempted to write a mathematical proof.

2. I challenged his assumption about a number n not being divisible by a number greater than n divided by 2.

Maybe not taking things for granted in a face-to-face interview is a good strategy?

Finally, I had my last interview with the test manager. He asked me the "four jars" testing question, which I had never heard before.

You have four jars containing pills. Three jars contain good pills, weighing 10 grams, but one jar contains bad pills, weighing 11 grams. It is a fact that a jar either contains all bad pills or all good pills. You have one scale. How many times do you need to weigh pills on the scale to determine which jar has the bad pills?

After a few iterations of breaking down the permutations on the whiteboard, I figured out the problem. We chatted briefly about how finding the fewest steps possible to determining a fact related to software testing, since everything you do, every time you weigh a pill, comes with some cost. As the interview continued, he talked about life on campus and the various people on his team. And next thing I knew, I got excited and watched myself shoot up in my chair and start working again on the problem, saying, "You *can* do it the way I described.

Here's how ..." and showed him my solution. Then I went pale, realizing what I had done. I turned around and frantically apologized for interrupting him. I'll never forget the smirk on his face when he said, "It's okay." All I could say was, "Sorry, the problem was still running on the background thread. It happens a lot," scratching the back of my head.

He just laughed, and the rest is history, as illustrated in this book.

Tip 252: You Can Make the Statement Completion Window Transparent

> **Sara Aside:** Wow! Hey, thank you for reading all the way to the end! About once or twice a year, whenever I write long conference trip reports or long summary e-mail messages at work, I usually have a line at the bottom saying, "To show my appreciation to you for reading this far, I'll buy you a latte. E-mail me to receive your coupon." It's fun to see people's reactions in their replies. In lieu of espresso, my way of saying thanks is to provide you with one last tip about Visual Studio 2008.

Hold down the Ctrl key to make the statement completion window transparent. This transparency is especially useful when the statement completion window is blocking text or other code that you need to read in order to know which object or method to select. And to make the statement completion window reappear, simply release the Ctrl key.

Index

X

About the Author

Photo courtesy of Microspotting.com

Sara Ford is the program manager for CodePlex, Microsoft's open source project hosting site. Prior to CodePlex, she worked on the Visual Studio team for six years, where she started the Visual Studio Tip of the Day on her blog. She began her career as a software design engineer in testing, where over the next four years she tested nearly every aspect of the generic Visual Studio IDE.

Shortly after the Visual Studio 2005 product shipped, Sara joined the Visual Studio Community Team as the program manager for Power Toys for Visual Studio. The power toys are small, lightweight add-ins to Visual Studio that were built as open-source projects on CodePlex. This is where her interests and personal education in the open-source world began, which would lead her to her current role on CodePlex.

It is a little-known fact that Sara ran a professional clown business named "Squirt, the Clown" (pronounced "Squirt Comma the Clown") throughout her junior high and high school years, where she juggled clubs and a diabolo and also twisted balloon animals. It turned out that the comma in the name was extremely important to clarify any confusion about the nature of her business. When Sara had been a professional clown for approximately two years, she arrived at a gig—a 10-year-old boy's birthday party—to find that the large group of boys (30, at least) were *over the top* excited to see the clown. She couldn't help but think their level of excitement was unusual for a group of that age. Then she noticed … they were all holding water guns! The boys opened fire, and the oversized clown shoes prevented her from making a hasty escape to her car. The parents, bless their hearts, took the original business name *"Squirt the Clown"* quite literally. Sara swears to this day that her life is the mathematical proof of Murphy's Law.

Aside from her clown business, Sara has had other interesting jobs as a soccer referee and a popcorn vendor at Walt Disney World, in the Magic Kingdom, directly in front of Cinderella's castle. When not working on a computer or running away from water guns, Sara enjoys studying Shotokan Karate, hiking mountains twice in a row, and cycling on trails that do not allow cars.

Sara's life long goal is to become a 97-year-old weightlifter, so she can be featured on the local news.

What do you think of this book?

We want to hear from you!

Your feedback will help us continually improve our books and learning resources for you. To participate in a brief online survey, please visit:

microsoft.com/learning/booksurvey

...and enter this book's ISBN-10 or ISBN-13 number (appears above barcode on back cover). As a thank-you to survey participants in the U.S. and Canada, each month we'll randomly select five respondents to win one of five $100 gift certificates from a leading online merchant. At the conclusion of the survey, you can enter the drawing by providing your e-mail address, which will be used for prize notification only.*

Thank you in advance for your input!

Where to find the ISBN on back cover

ISBN-13: 000-0-0000-0000-0
ISBN-10: 0-0000-0000-0

9 0 0 0 0

0 000000 000000

Example only. Each book has unique ISBN.

***Microsoft**® Press*

Stay in touch!

To subscribe to the *Microsoft Press® Book Connection Newsletter*—for news on upcoming books, events, and special offers—please visit:

microsoft.com/learning/books/newsletter